SILKSHEEN
The History of East Kirkby Airfield

Geoff D. Copeman

D1462868

DONCASTER LIBRARY AND INFORMATION SERVICE	
3O122O1874927 1	
Askews	3 1 JAN 2002
94O·544	£6.95
COP	

Copyright © 1989 & 1993
Geoff D. Copeman and
Midland Counties Publications.

First published in 1989 by
Midland Counties Publications,
24 The Hollow, Earl Shilton, Leicester
LE9 7NA, England.

Second (revised) edition 1993

ISBN 0 904597 84 9

All rights reserved. No part of this
publication may be reproduced, stored
in a retrieval system, transmitted in any
form or by any means, electronic,
mechanical or photo-copied,
recorded or otherwise, without the written
permission of the copyright owners.

Printed in England by
Printhaus Book Company Limited,
Northampton.

2

Contents

Front Cover, taken from a photograph:
Lancaster over Old Bolingbroke Windmill
in wartime. Mill House was the home of the
Elys who welcomed the RAF (Edna M. Ely).

Back Cover Photograph:
NX611's Cockpit section, sporting the
badge of Bomber Command, during
reassembly at East Kirkby. (W. J. Taylor).

Introduction

'Silksheen' was a code-word, chosen during the Second World War as the call-sign for Flying Control at East Kirkby, one of the RAF's 'temporary' bomber airfields in Lincolnshire. To the crews joining the circuit after hours of darkness, noise and fear, perhaps struggling to keep a damaged aircraft aloft over the North Sea, the calm voice, usually of a WAAF: 'Silksheen to...., you are clear to land. Runway Two' the word became synonymous with home.

Much has been written on the strategies of Britain's Bomber Offensive of the Second World War and many of the more spectacular achievements have been well recorded. Less attention has been paid to the efforts of what might be called 'the ordinary crews' and to the men and women supporting them. At the time, publicity ran a poor second to security, except where it might be used for propaganda or as a boost to morale, and when the job was finished most of the temporary airfields were closed with no more ceremony than when they were opened.

Soon forgotten too, were the local communities who welcomed and gave support to those who created such turmoil in their rural peace. East Kirkby still bears more scars than benefits from the intrusion but bears them with some pride. Few holidaymakers heading for the coast have given a second glance to this little village, unaware of the part it and many like it played in Hitler's downfall.

I hope that *Silksheen* may give a picture of how the lives of ordinary people, in or out of uniform, were changed by extraordinary circumstances, place on record the airfield's own history and provide an introduction to more recent developments in the village and at the airfield, now becoming an important local historical and tourist centre with the establishment of the new museum.

To critics who have chosen (Allied) bombing raids as the subject for condemnation from their soap boxes, perhaps the best reply is to paraphrase the response that was used to explain all short-comings between 1939 and 1945: 'Don't you know there was a war on?'

Geoff D. Copeman   November 1988
Baldock, Herts

This second edition of *Silksheen* gives a welcome opportunity to put right some errors and omissions and to thank readers kind enough to draw my attention to them. It has also made it possible to give an update on the development of the Heritage Centre. History doesn't stand still, for in July 1992 came news of the re-formation of No.57 Squadron at Lyneham, when Hercules training under 242 OCU adopted the identity of a famous squadron in reserve status and became the responsibility of No.57 (Reserve) Squadron.

Geoff D. Copeman   March 1993

Acknowledgements

Acknowledgments are due to the following among so many, many more: F.T.Bailey, L.Barnes, Messrs G.Bateman & Son (Wainfleet), R.N.E.Blake (for the map), D.Brown, A.E.de Bruin, W.Bullock, J.Chatterton, K.Coldron, D.Cooper, H.B.Crawford, Mrs E.M.Ely, J.P.Elliott, Mr & Mrs J.Garraway, C.Grebby, P.H.T.Green, G.Hall, Mr & Mrs W.Handson, M.J.Hodgson, W.Horsman, D.Howell, F.Jones, R.Jones, A.Leyva, H.le Marchant, J.Monk, T.Raines, J.Revell, A.H.Ricketts, Mrs K.Rowland (formerly Seward), W.J.Taylor, L.G.Wakerell, R.Witham, Messrs Woodroffe Walter (Horncastle), and to Miss Eileen Baker for help with the typing. Thanks are also due to the staff of Air Historical Branch (RAF), Imperial War Museum, Lincolnshire Archives Office, Newspaper Library, Public Record Office, RAF Museum Library.

Official Sources used (all 'Air' refer- ences, held at the Public Record Office, Kew): 8-1286, 14-2192, 25-122, 25-123, 27-537, 27-538, 27-539, 27-540, 27-541, 27-542, 27-2152, 27-2153, 29-854.

Abbreviations

AA	Anti-aircraft (Ack-ack)	NAAFI	Navy, Army & Air Forces Institute
AFC	Air Force Cross	NCO	Non-Commissioned Officer
AG	Air Gunner	NFT	Night Flying Test
AOC	Air Officer Commanding	OC	Officer Commanding
ATC	Air Training Corps	ORB	Operations Record Book
BEM	British Empire Medal	OTU	Operational Training Unit
CO	Commanding Officer	P/O	Pilot Officer
Cpl	Corporal	PX	Post Exchange
DFC	Distinguished Flying Cross	RAAF	Royal Australian Air Force
DFM	Distinguished Flying Medal	RCAF	Royal Canadian Air Force
DI	Daily Inspection	RNZAF	Royal New Zealand Air Force
DSO	Distinguished Service Order	R/T	Radio Telephone
F/O	Flying Officer	SAAF	South African Air Force
F/Lt	Flight Lieutenant	SAC	Strategic Air Command
F/Sgt	Flight Sergeant	Sgt	Sergeant
GD	General Duties	S/Ldr	Squadron Leader
GP	General Purpose	TI	Target Indicator
i/c	in charge	USAAF	United States Army Air Force
intercom	intercommunication (acft)	USAF	United States Air Force
LAC/LACW	Leading Aircraftsman/woman		(post-war)
MAP	Ministry of Aircraft Production	VC	Victoria Cross
MBE	Member of the British Empire	WAAF/Waaf	Womens' Auxiliary Air Force
MO	Medical Officer	W/Op	Wireless Operator
MT	Mechanical Transport	WO	Warrant Officer
MUG	Mid-upper Gunner	W/Cdr	Wing Commander

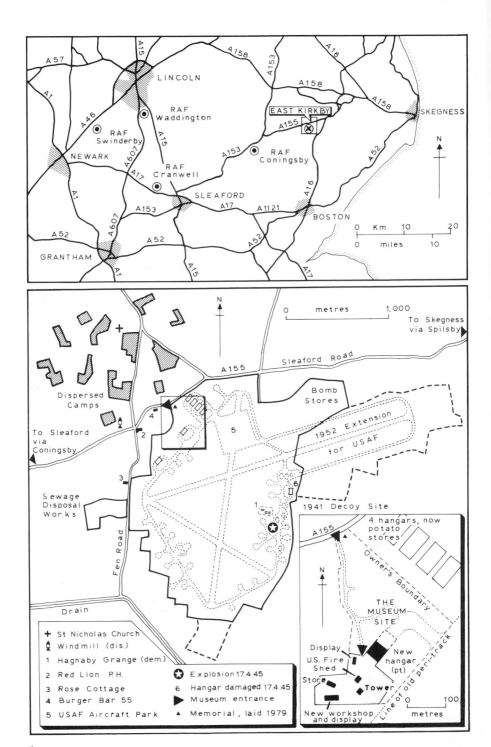

Upper map (regional):

A57 · A15 · A158 · A153 · A16 · A1 · A46 · LINCOLN · A158 · SKEGNESS

⊙ RAF Waddington · A15 · A158 · EAST KIRKBY ⊗ · A155

⊙ RAF Swinderby · A607 · A15 · A153 · A52

NEWARK · A17 · RAF Cranwell ⊙ · A153 · ⊙ RAF Coningsby · A16

A1 · A607 · SLEAFORD · A17 · A1121 · BOSTON

A52 · A153 · A52 · A52

GRANTHAM · A607 · A52 · A15 · A17

N

| 0 | Km | 10 | 20 |
| 0 | miles | | 10 |

Lower map (airfield):

N

| 0 | metres | 1,000 |

To Skegness via Spilsby ▶

Dispersed Camps

St Nicholas Church +

A155 · Sleaford Road

Bomb Stores

1952 Extension for USAF

To Sleaford via Coningsby ◀

4 · 2

Sewage Disposal Works

3

5

6 · 1941 Decoy Site

Fen Road

1 ⊡

☆

Drain

Legend:

✝ St Nicholas Church
⚑ Windmill (dis.)
1 Hagnaby Grange (dem.)
2 Red Lion P.H.
3 Rose Cottage
4 Burger Bar 55
5 USAF Aircraft Park

☆ Explosion 17.4.45
6 Hangar damaged 17.4.45
▶ Museum entrance
▲ Memorial, laid 1979

Inset (museum site):

4 hangars, now potato stores

A155

Owner's Boundary

N

THE MUSEUM SITE

Display
U.S. Fire Shed
Store

New hangar (pt)

Tower

Line of old peri-track

New workshop and display

| 0 | | 100 |
| | metres | |

Chapter One

East Kirkby and its Airfield

For years Britain had been warned that the looming war would be fought on the 'Home Front' and by the time 'the balloon went up' in 1939 few were inclined to disagree. In less than a year, many, particularly in the south, found themselves in the firing line.

For many rural communities further north, what became known as the phoney war lasted a bit longer, apart from the initial, sometimes painful, experiences as hosts to evacuees from the cities. In those early days rationing was not too stringent and the blackout no great hardship where street lighting was non-existent. The villagers had always led a simple life and it was natural to carry on, not that the heartache was any less for those with menfolk away fighting battles that too often seemed to be lost almost before they had started. As the war went on, however, many villages found their lives turned upside down in a way few could have foreseen and for some the changes became permanent.

One such is East Kirkby, lying just below the southernmost point of the Lincolnshire Wolds. Home in pre-war days for a couple of hundred souls, the village lies where the A155 Sleaford/Spilsby road is crossed by a minor road which emanates from Boston by way of Stickney before wandering north-west to Miningsby and Horncastle. Half a mile east along the main road another lane runs to join the Miningsby road and there behind the trees is the parish church of St Nicholas, the 'kirk' the village was 'by' before Britain was struck by plague - the 'Black Death' of 1348 - and the earlier dwellings were abandoned. Further east along the Spilsby road, Hagnaby Priory lies to the right amid the hamlet that housed the Squire's workers. From close by, in pre-war days, yet another lane wended its way southwards across the fields past a thatched cottage where lived the Head Gardener, and Hagnaby Grange Farm, thence by Staunch Farm or left down Back Lane, either way leading to the Stickney road.

In 1940 the Air Ministry was intent on establishing a number of 'decoy' aerodromes around the country to divert enemy bombers from their targets. Fields to the south of East Kirkby (actually in the parish of Hagnaby - population, 47) were ideally situated, lying as they did between the sea and such well-established bomber bases as Waddington and Scampton. The Ministry took a few fields near Back Lane and by grubbing out the hedges one of these 'K' Sites, as they were known, was soon prepared. Huts were built near the outlying cottages of Stickney village to house the specially trained airmen who were to operate the site and a worn out fire tender and ambulance added to the effect. For rations, pay, and so on, the site was under control of Coningsby though this nearby airfield did not commence bomber operations until the following year.

Shrouded in mystery and considered very 'hush-hush', the decoy naturally aroused curiosity in the locality. Each evening, as he dispensed cattle-cake to the stock in nearby fields, farmer's son John Chatterton viewed the activities with interest as the petrol driven generator was started and various flarepaths were tested. Later, he was surprised to see most realistic 'Whitley bombers' being assembled. These were, in fact, the product of film studios, masters in the creation of things that were not always what they appeared.

Operation of the decoy began on receipt of a 'Red Alert', signifying that enemy aircraft were in the vicinity. The flarepath appropriate to the wind direction would be switched on and the machine guns manned. Among the score or so who formed the Hagnaby crew was LAC Geoff Hall, a man endowed with an above average memory, for he still remembers most of their neighbours in the nearby cottages - and a lot of the girls! 'On top of the air-raid shelter was a small searchlight, operated by LAC Field and myself. During a Red Alert this light had to be directed onto whichever flarepath was being used and bounced up and down to represent a plane landing. Mind you, this became a bit frightening at times but proved its worth, for we were bombed on a number of occasions. Then, at daybreak, out came the shovels and barrows to fill in the craters. Next, all the Whitleys had to be moved around in case they had been photographed. This went on for over a year'. An aprocryphal story has it that closure followed a raid in which a German bomber dropped wooden bombs!

Time came when Britain began to fight back in the only way available, by bombing Germany. As Bomber Commmand gained strength, a massive programme of airfield construction was put in hand. The result was the most remarkable feat of civil engineering to be undertaken in this country in modern times, the more so bearing in mind that so many able-bodied men were in the armed forces and equipment was less sophisticated than now. During the war over five hundred new airfields were built, mostly down the eastern flank of England, and Lincolnshire received the lion's share, over fifty[1].

By mid-1942, No.5 Bomber Group, based almost entirely in the county, surpassed the strength of Bomber Command at the outbreak of the war. In a strip fifteen miles wide from the Trent to the coast ten bomber fields were in operation or nearing completion. There was room for a few more and the Ministry remembered the flat fields of Hagnaby.

They took this time a parcel of land, well over 800 acres (324 hectares), between East Kirkby and the old K Site, much of it belonging to Hagnaby Grange Farm. The larger part of the village, which, in truth, is not very extensive even today, lies in the eastern segment of the crossroads. Most of the technical buildings, the largest of which were the two T2 type hangars flanking the control Tower, were built closely behind this part of the village. Workshops, stores and offices, numbering about sixty, with as many again smaller huts, were spread along the side of the A155, extending almost to the Priory. A nearby stream was ducted underground and most of the road to Back Lane was swept away. The part that was left ran by a small belt of trees with the charming name 'The Solitude' which now seemed less than apt, for the new neighbours were to be the blast walls of the Bomb Store built behind the Priory.

The runway pattern conformed to the Ministry's Class 'A' Standard. Two 1,400 yard runways formed a 'V', converging on the Stickney road. They were crossed by the main runway of 2,000 yards running a little east of north towards a windmill on the hill that marked the beginning of the Wolds. This mill at Old Bolingbroke was still working through the war and became a much-loved landmark to the crews who flew from the airfield - some pilots claimed that their slipstream spurred 'the old girl' into greater activity! The mill proved to be a great attraction to many of the people on the station, especially those from overseas, and they were always made very welcome by Mr & Mrs Ely who lived there.

The perimeter track linking the runways had an unusual feature which made it popular with pilots in that apart from a gentle curve around the gardener's cottage each section was straight. This was a great advantage when heavy aircraft were being taxied for constant changes of direction by juggling throttles and brakes

[1] A Parliamentary Report issued in 1947 showed that between 1939 and 1945, 430 airfields suitable for bombers were built for the RAF and USAAF at a cost of £570m. The total area of concrete was 36,000 acres, about equal to the area of Edinburgh at that time.

The Red Lion, East Kirkby's only public house, as it was in pre-war days. Dispersal points occupied by 630 Squadron's Lancasters were to be built just beyond the paddock to the right *(Mrs I. Handson)*

The village butcher's shop was an integral part of the pub. Landlord Walter Handson displays a good stock of home-killed pork *(Mrs I. Handson)*

would invariably lead to overheated engines and loss of pneumatic brake pressure. Dispersed around the track were the hardstandings for the aircraft and near Grange Farm a third hangar was erected.

The Chatterton family and their forebears had once worked Old Bolingbroke mill as well as the red brick mill that had spread its six sails near the crossroads. They turned from milling and farmed Hagnaby Grange until shortly before the war, retaining only some grazing near Back Lane when they moved. By 1943 John Chatterton was in the RAF himself, learning to fly in Arizona. To keep him in touch with local developments and yet defeat the postal censor his mother devised a simple code, thus: 'There are no stock on the old farm at present but we hear they are getting some black bullocks soon'. Even as Mrs Chatterton wrote, the farmhouse was being reduced to a ruin, the doors and floorboards taken to kindle the contractors' tea kettles.

Not that tea was the only tipple, for the Red Lion in the village was soon busier than ever before or since. To meet the demands of the hard working, hard drinking navvies, the brewers delivered a weekly supply of thirty 18-gallon 'kils' of bitter and, giving a clue as to the origins of most of the customers, 200 dozen half pint bottles of Guinness!

The Red Lion was the village's only pub and was one of those splendid institutions, alas no longer to be found, for one room was set aside as the butcher's shop, while at the rear was a slaughterhouse. Another outhouse was the 'sausage room' where, during the occupation by 'Laing's Army', landlord/butcher Walter Handson was at work before dawn each day producing a hundredweight of sausages to feed the 'troops'.

Of an evening, the one room of the licensed premises soon filled up and latecomers had to stand shoulder to shoulder in the entrance passage where the little bar was sited, serving directly from the cellar. With no beer pumps to speed the service, the only way in which the supply of draught beer could meet demand was by opening the tap on the cask and letting it trickle continuously into a bucket, from which it was scooped by the glass. It was found prudent to charge a shilling (5p) deposit on each glass to reduce breakages and avoid the predicament of another 'local' which had to resort to 1lb and 2lb jam jars.

To comply with the strict wartime regulations, any visitor staying over-night at the Red Lion had to register. An arrival in August 1942 gave rise to a 'spy scare' in the village. A young woman with a rich brogue turned up, seeking a room whilst she visited a friend working on the 'drome', as it was called. She needed help in registering and when she recorded her nationality as 'British', the landlord laughed: "With an accent like that?" Bridget Mary amended the entry to 'Irish'. Next day, the police arrived to examine the register. They had arrested Bridget on the airfield for taking photographs and had confiscated her camera. What became of the 'special agent' with her photos of secret concrete mixers is not recorded.

The area of concrete on the airfield itself approached one hundred acres and this work, with the necessary levelling, drainage, underground cables and the sunken lights for perimeter track and runways accounted for almost half of the £1,000,000 sterling each of these airfields was expected to cost. In comparison, the latest pre-war figures available show the rateable values of East Kirkby and Hagnaby to be £3,260 and £1,200 respectively. Just as one side of the village was all but overwhelmed by the technical site, so the rest was soon surrounded as the living sites and other accommodation was erected, each larger, and to have a population greater than the village.

As one looks more closely at the problems faced by the engineers who designed the wartime aerodromes one is bound to admire the way in which they achieved the finished result, which matched aircraft performance to the prevailing wind and local topography. To add to their difficulties, of course, everything was carried out in a race against the clock, despite shortages of man-power and materials. Every day brought a new question to answer. As construction of the airfield neared completion necessary refinements had to be considered. Regulations required that tall buildings be topped by a red 'obstruction light', (Lincoln Cathedral being the county's most prominent example, in every sense). The same rules applied to buildings within 15 degrees either side of each runway approach. Here, what was called the '1 in 50 rule' was applied, comparing the height of a building to its distance from the runway's end. Nine hundred feet from the WSW end of No.6 runway stood Rose Cottage, Fen Road, just within the angle. At that distance a building higher than 18 feet required a light. However, adjacent to the cottage and just outside the angle stood a belt of trees, 70 to 80 feet high and much more dangerous. There was much discussion before it was decided that a light on the cottage might be misleading and the regulations were waived.

In the triangle formed by the roads running down to the church, Station Headquarters and the Operations Block took up the most central position. By each of the two roads communal sites were built and here were located the Dining Halls, Shower Blocks and the NAAFI Institutes. On the larger of the two, 'No.1 Site' – situated on Church Road in front of Manor Farm, were the Officers' and Sergeants' Messes and a large gymnasium that doubled as a chapel. Behind the farm were Nos 3 and 4 Sites, built on very uneven pasture land. Some huts were of the prefabricated 'Seco' variety whilst others were 'Nissens'. As they were dispersed at random their foundations provided plenty of work for bricklayers, one course of bricks at one side or end and ten at the other being the norm. The Messes, offices, etc, were all of the larger Nissen pattern, officially 'Romneys'. The gym and smaller buildings, such as the numerous ablutions and latrines, were generally of brick and breeze block construction, rendered with cement, asbestos-roofed, and painted the colour of new-mown hay.

At Woodbine Cottage, next door to her father's Smithy, lived Edna Vickers. She was the village dairymaid and well recalls the abrupt manner in which the requisitioned land was taken, for she saw hedges and gates torn out around her cows as they grazed.

Forty per cent of the living accommodation was allocated to officers and sergeants, which gives an idea of the aircrew establishment of a heavy bomber station of the time. Each crew comprised the Pilot, (usually, but not always, the captain), Flight Engineer, Navigator, Wireless Operator, Air Bomber, (invariably referred to as the Bomb-aimer), and the Mid-upper and Rear Gunners, who were interchangeable in theory but seldom in practise.

For every man in the air, three or four men or women were required for technical support. Additionally, the Station staff to provide administration, supplies, etc and the 'domestic' support would run into hundreds.

By August 1943, the contractors' workforce began to move on to their next task and the Red Lion reverted to the eight dozen Guinness that fulfilled normal weekly needs. On the 19th, Headquarters staff for the embryo station began to move in. Soon the roads were alive with traffic and Edna Vickers had to learn the art of guiding her charges through equally wayward herds of airmen.

On the 20th the RAF Ensign was flying as the first Station Commander took over. Group Captain R.T. Taffe OBE was a man held in high regard by those who served under him. In due course the aircrews would welcome his customary visits to their Briefing, when he would deliver a few words of encouragement, sometimes a little joke, and finally: "Good luck, gentlemen, and good bombing!"

In a rudimentary fashion the Station was a small town, introducing amenities new to the district - flush sanitation for one. Essential work was by no means complete but the remaining quarters were soon to be occupied. East Kirkby was going to war.

'On the circuit'. A Lancaster passes Old Bolingbroke Mill, then home of the Ely family. *(Mrs E.M. Ely)*

Badge of 57 Squadron. The motto translates as 'The body changes, not the spirit'.

'Fifty-seven Anonymous', though the heavy deposits of lead behind the exhausts indicate a veteran *(Imperial War Museum CH 12971)*

Chapter Two

Moving In

No heavy bomber can have been talked and written of as much as the Avro Lancaster. More than forty years after its inception the affection generated among those whose cause it served shows little sign of waning. Without attempting to belittle the work of the aircraft that bore the brunt in the early days – or nights – of the bomber offensive, there can be no doubt that the 'Lanc' was a war plane in a class of its own.

For just a year after joining 5 Group to convert from Wellingtons to Lancasters, No.57 Squadron had operated from the grass airfield at Scampton. They had played a significant part in the formation of the soon famous No.617 Squadron and had lost some of their most experienced crews on the 'Dams' raids. Since then, the two Squadrons had flown on operations together but flying from Scampton now had to cease whilst concrete runways were laid and the units were to be posted – 'The Dambusters' to Coningsby, 'The Heinz Varieties' to an airfield they had never heard of – East Kirkby.

The Order for the impending move came just as Wing Commander H.W.F. Fisher DFC assumed command of 57. It stated that two days were to be allowed for the process of movement and was adamant: 'In no circumstances is the move to be allowed to interfere with the Squadron's operational requirements'. Despite this, the Order concluded with the reminder: 'The customary Parade and Inspection on leaving the old Station and again on arrival at the new are to be carried out in accordance with King's Regulations'.

It was a challenge and the Squadron rose to it. On the morning of 27th August

1943, as the bombers landed at Scampton from a raid an advance party left for the new Station. The Lancasters were swiftly serviced and made the short transfer flight, soon to be followed by the rest of the Squadron personnel, over 900 in all.

The newcomers, accustomed to the pre-war comforts of Scampton's polished barrack blocks, viewed with some exprobation the bare huts with the old-fashioned coke stoves after picking their way through the mud so synonymous with dispersed living sites. But there was not time for settling in; first must come the mammoth task of dealing with the tons of tools, spares and equipment.

By the afternoon of the 30th the aircraft were fuelled and bombed-up. The fourteen crews detailed for East Kirkby's first war operation assembled in candle-light, the Briefing Room not yet being connected to the mains, and duly took off to attack Mönchengladbach. All returned safely.

The second raid, on Berlin, took place on 3rd/4th September. Again fourteen crews took part but this time one failed to return. Squadron strength continued to increase, however, and twenty-two planes made the journey to Hanover and back. Whatever the truth regarding the last attack on the K-Site, it soon became obvious that the enemy knew exactly what was going on the in Hagnaby fields now, for as the bombers reached home a German nightfighter joined them on the circuit. A 'Scram' signal went out from Flying Control as the runway lights were switched off, but for 57's 'S-Sugar', the warning came too late; the crew were unaware of the danger until cannon shells tore into their plane - two crew escaping by parachute.

'Bottle Party' in the Sergeants' Mess during a stand-down midway through the Battle of Berlin, 1943/44.
(D. Cooper)

Five days later, Squadron Leader Malcolm Crocker DFC was OC Ops and called for his bomb-aimer, Harry Le Marchant, also 'Duty Dog', about an hour before the bombers were due back. As they climbed into the little Standard van – a Flight Commander's 'perks' - they heard a curious aircraft sound in the distance. They decided it sounded like twin engines slightly out of synchronisation, a German habit, and reported their suspicions on arrival at the Control Tower. Several returning bombers were attacked near their bases that morning and a 'Bandit' was shot down over The Wash, but at East Kirkby the Scram warning was timely and the Lancasters were diverted to Waterbeach. They came home next day but as 'V-Victor' came into view watchers could see that two of her engines were feathered and looked on in horror as she sank to crash on the hill. Three of her crew were killed. Mrs Chatterton duly reported: 'The black bullocks have arrived on the farm but one or two have died rather suddenly'.

Station Sick Quarters were situated in a field beyond Kirkby Mill and at this time there was no part set aside as a 'Crash

Area', able to deal with a number of casualties at one time. Throughout that first winter the Station Medical Officer complained of the conditions in which he was expected to provide a hospital for 2,000 people on a war footing - and, such is human nature, there was the rare occasion when maternity facilities were required! In time, the MO's efforts met with some success, for he was able to report that by boarding up unglazed windows he had been able to prepare two wards, one for airmen, one for WAAF. There was, however, only one bed in each! He also reported that a number of 'well proven' remedies to eliminate dust from the bare concrete floors had been tried without success.

The Squadron carried out an attack on Mannheim on 23rd September. The aircraft began to land from 01.55 hours onwards next morning, but of 'G-George' there was no sign and the Operations

Record Book was endorsed with the all too-frequent entry: 'Not heard of again'. However, the circumstances surrounding the loss of this aircraft led to an interesting sequel years later. At about one o'clock in the morning of the 24th, 'DX-G' flew over the north-eastern suburbs of Paris. Though no air raid warning had been sounded people soon woke to the sound of anti-aircraft fire and watched as search-lights and tracer shells swept the sky. The battery located at the Pré-Saint-Gervais soon found their target and the plane was seen to be on fire for sometime it circled at about 500 feet then gradually lost height, heading for the Seine.

The Watch Office — 'Silksheen'.
'Met Man' Fg Off Pat Doherty (centre) discusses the weather situation with the Station Commander, Gp Capt Taafe. Behind them can be seen an indicator board showing that the 2/5 runway (080°-260°) is illuminated. On the desk is a panel marked 'Intruders', used to initiate 'Scram' action *(IWM)*

The firemen of the J.J. Rousseau Station heard the guns and the drone of the air-craft. Suddenly, the plane roared low over the station and a loud explosion shook the ground. They turned out to attend the inci-dent and found wreckage scattered over a wide area. The fuselage and starboard wing had fallen on the roof of the Magasins du Louvre, setting fire to it, whilst the rear turret lay in front of a cafe on the corner of the rue du Louvre and the rue du Rivoli. All those aboard had died instantly and local folk who arrived at the scene observed that none wore a parachute, a fact which tended to confirm the view expressed by many that the crew had sacrificed them-selves in an attempt to reach the river and prevent casualties among the civilian populace.

Soon after the war a plaque was erected nearby to honour Flying Officer J.D. Hogan, RCAF, and his gallant crew and a simple act of remembrance has been held there on each anniversary.

As the fortieth anniversary approached, many Parisiens who recalled the event expressed the wish that the occasion be

marked in some more tangible form and the city decided to bestow a gold medal, its highest honour, on No.57 Squadron. At a special ceremony held at the Hotel de Ville on 24th November 1983, the Mayor of Paris's Fourth Arrondissement, M Pierre-Charles Kreig, himself a witness to the tragedy, presented the Grande Medaille de la Ville de Paris to the current Commanding Officer, Wing Commander Alan Bowman MBE, to honour the Squadron and its members who had paid the sacrifice so long ago.

Returning to September 1943, none of the crews had had long to become familiar with the area surrounding their new airfield and as the nights drew in some found it difficult to locate. To add to the confusion, tests were being carried out on the 'Drem' system lighting of two more new airfields, one at nearby Spilsby and another at Strubby, fourteen miles to the north-east. Harry Le Marchant recalls one night as they returned from ops: 'There was low cloud over East Kirkby. Flying Control has us 'stacked' well above earlier arrivals but we saw the lights through gaps in the cloud. Our turn to land arrived and as we broke cloud we had an excellent view and a perfect touchdown was effected. It was as we turned off the runway to trundle to our dispersal that the queries started: 'Don't remember this ... or that'. The faint but familiar voice of the 'Silksheen' Waaf came through: 'You've landed at Strubby'. Red faces all round; we were the first of many.'

The Squadron joined in attacks on Hanover on 8th/9th October and again on the 18th/19th. During the latter raid, despite severe injuries which included the loss of an eye, F/Sgt Walter Cowham, gunner aboard 'Y-Yoke', fought off continuing attacks by fighters. For this action he was awarded an immediate Conspicuous Gallantry medal – the non-commissioned airman's 'DSO'.

Over and above the need to replace 'wastage', new crews, including a leavening of experienced men from other squadrons continued to be posted in. On 15th November, the whole of 'B' Flight was elevated to become No.630 Squadron, the Flight Commander, Squadron Leader Crocker, an American, being promoted to lead the new unit.

For some weeks the infant squadron suffered shortages of all kinds, along with the discomforts they shared with their colleagues of 57. In the Officers' Quarters, four batmen had to 'do' for forty officers in huts devoid of furniture other than beds and without floor covering or even coat hooks. Six-thirty's Operations Record Book complains with some feeling that toilet blocks were just as the builders had left them and the nearest facilities were 200 yards from the Squadron offices. The earliest entries in the Operations Record Book were handwritten and it was some weeks before the first typed report appeared, concluding with the triumphant note: 'Posted in: Clerk, GD, WAAF, able to type.'

Despite the shortages, crews, aircraft and adaptability were abundant, and on 18th November, just three days after formation, 630's new Lancasters were carrying their code letters 'LE' out over the North Sea to Berlin. One of No. 57's Lancasters crashed on take-off that night, killing three of the crew, and another failed to return. Six-thirty suffered their first losses on the 23rd, when two of their crews were posted missing after the Squadron's third attack on the German capital.

December began badly, for each unit lost two crews on the night of 3rd/4th. AVM The Hon R.A. Cochrane CBE AFC, Air Officer Commanding No.5 Group, made his first visit to the Station early in the month. Tour expired, Wing Commander Crocker handed over his command to Wing Commander Rollinson on the 13th.

A Lancaster of 106 Squadron reported a 'ditched' aircraft as she returned from Berlin on the morning of the 17th but when the minesweeper *Typhoon* arrived on the scene only the wireless operator of 57's 'N-Nan' had survived.

By this time the Station had its own weekly magazine, *The Bull*, just one of the measures taken to create the right kind of atmosphere for living and working together. A Social Club was formed and each Sunday the 'All Hands Dance' proved popular, as

'Cookie', the 4,000 lbs High Capacity bomb. The narrow propeller blades of the Lancaster behind identify it as a Mk.III. *(Geoff D. Copeman)*

The Lancasters move round to the take-off point. *(D. Brown)*

did the weekly programmes of gramophone records, ranging from the classics to swing.

Preparations for the festive season had been in hand for some weeks. A toy making competition had been held in November and the entries provided a present for each child when a party was held on 21st December for the village children and the families of 'living-out' personnel. That evening, what was probably the biggest social event the district had seen for many a day took place in the form of the first Officers Mess party. AOC Group was Guest of Honour and the verdict was 'most successful'.

The war against Berlin continued though, and another of 57's crews was lost on the night of 23rd/24th.

When the more fortunate crews landed that morning, operations ceased for a few days and the seasonal celebrations were carried out in mostly, but not entirely, traditional manner. The officers served the other ranks with their turkey and free beer for Christmas lunch before returning to their Mess for afternoon tea. With axes 'borrowed' from the aircraft they had cut themselves logs and they settled before an open fire. Settled, that is, until someone bet a vivacious Intelligence Officer that she dare not throw an innocuous-looking paper bag on the fire. She accepted the bet, not knowing that it held the contents of several Very Pistol cartridges. Multi-coloured chaos followed as chairs, teacups and christmas cake were scattered across the carpet. Though the layer of 'strato-cu' persisted beneath the ceiling, the rest of the evening seemed set to pass sedately until a self-appointed Santa climbed onto the roof and clattered a handful of small change down a ventilation shaft.

Meanwhile, the rest of the camp enjoyed a cabaret and dance in No.2 Dining Hall. The fare served in that hall on Boxing Night, open to all ranks – and to any villagers with the inclination and ninepence (4p) to spare – was the Lamour/Crosby/Hope team on The Road to Morocco.

Despite the bad weather, time off was limited and 57 lost another aircraft before the year was out. On the evening of New Year's Day the Squadrons joined in a further assault on Berlin.

Six-Thirty's 'D-Dog' climbing hard into the evening sky. *(IWM)*

An
ADJUTANT'S
WARNING !

WHEN dicing in the upper air
At night my son, I pray take care
And ere you leave the flarepath's glow
Recite this charm before you go

"From Gremlins & Gremlets* & other strange beasties
And things that prang kites in the night,
Good Lord deliver us ! "

Keep out of clouds, watch out for ice,
Mark well the circuit as you dice :
Rely implicitly, O tyro,
Upon the reading of your gyro.

Remember this & other lore,
Drummed into your head before :
Apply with care all "gen" you know,
Land her safe, then taxy slow.

Guard your precious life, my son,
For once the damage has been done,
Your worry's o'er : You leave life's glamour –
But my work starts from there, O Pranger !

*
Small, immature Gremlins, usually born out of wedlock, found almost exclusively in the North of Scotland.

This warning which adorned the Adjutant's office in 630's HQ surely owes
either acknowledgement or apology to 'Raff' and Anthony Armstrong.

Chapter Three

1944 - First Quarter

Among a number of decorations awarded members of the Squadrons early in the New Year was a DSO to Squadron Leader J. Vivian DFC, a navigator with 57. Now posted to Group HQ as Navigation Officer, he had served as a Flight Commander and as an aircraft captain during his second tour. An immediate award of the DFC went to Pilot Officer J.B. Josling, with whom Vivian had flown a number of times. Josling joined 57 Squadron in May 1943, when just twenty years old and had shown great determination in overcoming the considerable difficulties that befell him – technical failures, icing and other adverse weather conditions and combinations of them all. Since May he had married, been commissioned and decorated, a pattern followed by so many young men at the time. But again so typically, fate held the last card and John Josling was killed in a flying accident the following summer.

To 630's first CO, Malcolm Crocker, went a Bar to the DFC awarded only months before – a unique distinction to have won the decoration with both 57 and 630. He too was to lose his life later in 1944 whilst in command of another squadron. An immediate award of the DFC also went to Flying Officer Erik Neils Westergaard, one of the few Danes to fly with Bomber Command. Yet again though, a sad end to the tale, for he did not live to see his country free.

The Lancasters carried the H2S radar scanner in the bulbous projection underneath, by means of which a 'picture' of coastal outlines, built-up areas, etc, could be seen on a screen. A modification was introduced to make use of part of the cone-like volume swept by the scanner to search for fighters lurking in the bomber's blind spot below. The system was known as 'Fishpond' and 57 were given the task of evaluating it. Through January they used it on their operations, the observation being an extra duty for the wireless operators. With practice, they became adept at interpreting the little 'blips' and their reports showed that combat had been avoided nine times on eighty sorties.

For the ground crews it was an unrelenting routine – the damage from the night before to be repaired and the 'DIs' (Daily Inspections) to be carried out before the Form 700, the Aircraft Serviceability Record, could be signed to certify that each task was complete, and all in a race against the clock as the next 'Maximum Effort' was laid on.

Along with the everyday chores, Roy Jones, an armourer, remembers the rare events: an electrician, carrying out a continuity check on the bomb release circuit, created a 'short' and the newly-loaded bombs dropped to the tarmac. On occasion, a Lancaster would return with a loose hang-up', a bomb rolling free in the bay. 'Removal', he says, 'was an operation guaranteed to clear that part of the airfield in double-quick time'.

As Operations Planning continued with their task of taking the war to the major cities of Germany, the weather loomed large in their calculations, for it could make or break an attack. Not so on the windswept airfields; aside from snow clearance, any effect the weather might have on daily maintenance was disregarded by the powers that be. 'The show must go on'.

It was a hard winter; small wonder that

the principal recollection of many is of 'the bitter wind, coming straight from Siberia'. Life on the Station became even more arduous at the end of the month for they were without hot or cold water for several days. Roy Jones, again: 'There were terribly cold mornings when the guns would stick to your hands. Sometimes our invaluable bikes were immobilised as the chain froze to the rear sprocket. I believe it was that cheeky, cheerful Londoner, Joe Craddock, who devised a remedy by peeing on it! It was a sight to behold: a line of propped-up bikes, a line of airmen and a lot of steam!

They were a great crowd, both at work and on 'stand-down nights' when we let our hair down at the local pub or in Boston. Our Sergeant, 'Jock' Webster, had the knack of being able to 'win' whatever we needed, whether from Stores or cookhouse – we always seemed to be hungry.

An affinity grew between ground staff and aircrew and there was a sadness and sense of loss when one of our kites failed to return. I was Duty Armourer one night early in 1944 when Berlin seemed to be the target every night. With all the duty crew in the small Flight Hut, the cigarette fug was as thick as usual, so I stepped outside for a breath of fresh air. It was a cold, clear night and as my eyes became accustomed to it I saw that a dispersal point left vacant by a loss a couple of nights before now had a Lancaster on it. I was surprised as there had been no 'early returns', so I walked over to check on what, or whose, plane it was. As I got nearer, it just vanished. I tried to convince myself it was a trick of the light or night, but when I returned to the spot where I had originally stood the dispersal was quite clearly empty.'

Empty dispersals were all too common, for nine crews were lost to the station during January, including 630's CO, Wing Commander Rollinson. The new, inexperienced crews now joining the Squadrons were certainly being 'thrown in the deep end'. Pilot Officer J. Castagnola began his tour with 57 with three trips to Berlin – a tour eventually completed with 617 Squadron. Les Barnes and his crew flew with 630 and visited Berlin for their first four ops: 'The third of these was a bit hairy; we were attacked over Magdeburg on the way home. 'Jerry' made a couple of passes, my gunners returned his fire and he broke away. My rear gunner claimed a hit as smoke was seen coming from the fighter. Safely home, we returned to the aircraft to assess the damage in daylight and arrived just as an unexploded cannon shell was being extracted from a starboard fuel tank.'

Now that Freya and Giant Würzburg radars extended right across Europe the 'Bombers' Moon' had become a thing of the past. Night-fighter pilots could excel at their art with the aid of a full moon so for these periods the bombing offensive slackened. There was not to be much time off for the aircrews in the 'moon period' of early February 1944, however, for Wing Commander Fisher and 630's new CO, Wing Commander W.I. Deas DFC, introduced 'special training'. Pilots and engineers attended lectures on engine handling, etc, and the latter spent some time in the hangars helping with overhauls. The biggest event of the stand down was an escape exercise in which aircrew were taken in closed vehicles and dropped seven or eight miles from camp. They had to find their way back, avoiding capture by a hundred or so of their colleagues, supposedly enemy troops. The finale of the week was a huge party, the aircrews playing host to their ground crews.

Tragedy came unexpectedly on 12th February, when Lancaster W4119, a veteran serving with 50 Squadron, caught fire in mid-air whilst on a training exercise. Without warning, she plunged through the thick cloud to crash on the edge of the airfield, near No.3 Hangar. Fortunately, five of those aboard were able to escape by parachute.

Though death became commonplace on bomber fields, sometimes there was added poignancy. Such was the case when Flying Officer E.J. Murray, RAAF, set off down the runway, Stuttgart-bound, on his first operation. Taking off with a full bomb load was the only exercise that could not be practised during training and the runways were scarcely long enough for a 29 ton Lancaster at the best of times. Murray's aircraft swung, and as it careered across the Stickney road the undercarriage collapsed. The bomb load exploded immediately, with a blast that broke windows in Skegness, fifteen miles away. Amazingly, the rear gunner was taken almost unhurt from his turret, one of the few parts of the plane found intact.

Les Barnes has his own reasons to remember that night: 'Stuttgart was our fifth operation and a surprise attack from below severed the hydraulics and put the turrets out of action. Further attacks were made and the rear gunner reported difficulties in returning fire. I sensed that he had been wounded and gave him permission to bale out, as I felt it was his only chance. I 'clocked up' 360 mph as I dived to 12,000 feet trying to shake the fighter off, unaware that the Lanc was on fire and we were a sitting duck. He hit both starboard engines and I gave the order to abandon the aircraft. Left alone with no time to spare, I made a headlong dive for the hatch in the nose. I missed and rolled over the bomb-sight, stunned. I came round somersaulting through the air and pulled the ripcord – twenty-three years later I learned from an eyewitness that the aircraft had exploded in mid-air.

Good fortune stayed with Barnes, for after hiding in a haystack for a few hours he made contact with the French Resistance and was set for a long, eventful, journey home.

No.5 Group was given a new role to play when ordered to attack industrial targets in France. As the objectives were often small and in closely built-up areas, accurate marking was vital and was almost invariably carried out by the Group's own Pathfinders from 54 Base at Coningsby.

Commitment to the specialised targets did not release the Group from playing its part in the Main Force raids. On the night of 15th February, 630 were able to claim to be the largest squadron in Bomber Command, sending twenty-one aircraft to the Reich capital. All returned safely, though one crashed on landing.

As Tony Leyva, a 630 navigator, left the Briefing Room on 24th March for another attack on 'The Big City', he looked suspiciously at his parachute pack. In the Parachute Section the assistants smiled as he told of his unfounded but nagging doubts. The 'chute was almost due for its regular airing and re-packing so, indulgently, they invited him to pull the ripcord. The counter became swathed in billowing silk and he murmured his embarrassed apologies as they gave him another pack, complete, as they always said, with guarantee: 'Bring it back if it doesn't work!'

Hours later, as Leyva worked over his charts, the aircraft rocked violently and the cabin was raked by cannon shells. The intercom was dead and as he reached for his 'chute he felt a blast of cold air from the front hatch. He thrust the pack up to the hooks on his chest just as the pilot, dead or wounded, fell forward over the controls and the plane roared into a power dive. Leyva was sent into a mad helter-skelter along the polished leather of his bench, down the cabin floor into the nose compartment and found himself falling through space. He pulled the rip-cord, but this time nothing happened. Frantically he tore at the flaps of the pack and suddenly a white streak flashed past his face and he was jerked into a lopsided suspension. Looking up he saw that only one of the two hooks was attached, but he landed safely. Quickly taken prisoner, he found he was the sole survivor. The bomb-aimer or the engineer must have opened the hatch. Had they both been thrown into the nose and trapped? At daybreak he was taken to where the wreck of the Lancaster lay in a bog. Still numb from shock, he gazed quite dispassionately at the burntout centre section and at the gunners who had been his friends, now dead in their turrets, before his captors led him away.

One of 57's wireless operators put his 'Fishpond' to good use that night. Seeing the wandering 'blip' of a fighter closing on the slower image of a bomber he directed his pilot and gunners so well that they were able to shoot the marauder down. This raid turned out to be the last of the series that came to be known as the Battle of Berlin and brought East Kirkby's saddest night to date, 57 and 630 losing two and three aircraft respectively.

The few months of action had blooded 630 Squadron and they rapidly found an identity of their own, friendly rivalry building up between the two units. When 57's CO, detecting a slackness among his men, instituted a temporary series of morning parades 630 were quick to seize the chance to dub them '57 ITW' - (Initial Training Wing), sweet revenge on those long-serving members of the senior squadron who still referred to 630 as 'C Flight'. Between ops every opportunity was taken to improve bombing accuracy and in March's Bombing Competition 57 seemed to be the Prodigal Son, being judged to have shown 'remarkable improvement to share fifth place', though 630 received no commendation for coming fourth!

Throughout the winter enemy defences had become increasingly successful – seventy-three bombers were lost on the last Berlin raid, Bomber Command's heaviest losses so far. But the worst was yet to come. On March 30th the target was Nuremburg and for the bombers it seemed nothing could go right. The new moon betrayed their condensation trails as the overcast weather cleared; the wind

The ground crew pass the long night hours away in the Flight Hut *(IWM)*

changed, causing the first wave to arrive late and the second early. The German controllers saw through every 'spoof' and diversion and even their own mistakes turned to their advantage.

When day broke, the enormity of the overnight events produced a trail of shattered nerves from Command HQ at High Wycombe to the smallest OTU. Of nearly eight hundred bombers, ninety-four had fallen and another dozen had crashed on return. In military terms, an unacceptable 11.8% missing rate; by any other terms, nearly seven hundred men would not be coming back.

All but one of 57's crews got home safely but, of 630's sixteen aircraft, three were lost. LE 'C-Charlie' had a lucky escape when, with rear guns frozen, a burst from the mid-upper caused a twin-engined fighter to break away. Two other gunners claimed to have destroyed a Junkers Ju 88 and damaged another.

Losses apart, the raid had not been as effective as might have been expected of a Main Force operation of major proportion and Bomber Command seemed to retire for a day or two to catch its breath. Strategic thinking underwent a review but the changes that followed were tactical and due to plans to use the bomber forces in preparation for the long awaited 'Second Front', the return to Northern Europe. A new phase was about to begin.

Chapter Four

Run-up to Invasion
April – June 1944

Within days East Kirkby was back in action; on the night of 5th/6th April, Wing Commander Fisher led the 5 Group attack on the airfield at Toulouse. There was a pause for Easter Sunday Church Parade, then raids on the railway yards at Tours and Aachen. On a free night the Waafs ran one of their popular dances in the Naafi – records, of course; *In the Mood, Whispering Grass* and plenty of Victor Sylvester.

Wing Commander H.Y. Humphreys DFC assumed command of No.57 Squadron on the 15th of April. On the same day, East Kirkby became a Base Station, No.55 Base, taking control of Spilsby and of No.207 Squadron which had operated from there since October 1943. From the first day, Spilsby had relied heavily on East Kirkby; now this support was the responsibility of the Base. In effect, elevation to Base status raised the Station HQ staff and it was, to a large extent, replacements for these people who were the newcomers. Additionally, the Base became responsible for the administration of the airfield at Strubby which opened on the same day. No.280 Squadron were to fly their Warwicks on Coastal Command duties from there very shortly.

From a technical outlook, the largest commitment was that the Base was to take over the major servicing of the Lancasters of the three squadrons. To this end, four additional hangars had been built during the winter. These stood side by side between the A155 and the perimeter track. Their construction and the provision of associated 'shooting-in butts' for test and alignment of gun turrets cost the Station three of its hardstandings. After protest, Works Dept agreed to provide two replacement 'loops' at an estimated cost of £6,000.

The bombers continued their attacks on railway yards, those on Juvisy and the Gare du Nord, La Chapelle, proving enormously successful and demonstrating the effectiveness of the marking schemes being evolved by the 5 Group Pathfinders. These were planned in such a way as to avoid the markers being 'bombed out' or obscured by smoke, and each time the target was hit and the nearby residential districts untouched.

Actually, on the first raid, one stick of bombs did miss the target and demolished a block of flats. As this happened to be the local headquarters of the German Army, the citizens of Juvisy credited the RAF bomb-aimers with a little more skill than they may have deserved! One of 57's aircraft, returning from this raid, crashed in Cambridgeshire and all on board were killed. Among them, as second pilot for his first operation, was Pilot Officer Culliford. Back at Base, his crew waited in vain but could only mourn the loss of their 'Aussie' skipper. The Squadron suffered a further blow when their 'A' Flight Commander, Squadron Leader P.M. Wigg, failed to return from La Chappelle.

The Squadrons visited Brunswick without loss on the 22nd, then before the shorter nights could put a stop to the long journeys made two 'maximum fuel' raids by way of south-west France. The first of these, an eleven hour slog to Munich, was said by experienced crews to be the best concentration of attack they had seen. The port inner engine of 630's 'G-George' caught fire that night and the pilot, Pilot Officer L.M. Rackley, decided to head for

Switzerland before baling out. Unable to gain enough height to clear the Alps, he turned towards the Mediterranean, where he found an airfield at Borgo, on the East coast of Corsica, freed by the French in the autumn. As he went in to land he lost two more engines and in the ensuing heavy landing 'George' swung, the tail hit another plane and the gunner was killed. Untypically, the record on this incident elicits only the comment that the gunner should not have been in his turret for an emergency landing.

The second of these long distance raids, aimed at Schweinfurt, ran late because of unexpectedly strong winds and the German controller, undeceived by spoof routes, soon got his 'bandits' into the stream of bombers. Of 296, twenty-three were lost that night, among them one from 630 and two from 57, including that flown by Squadron Leader M.I. Boyle, 'B' Flight Commander. Two other Lancasters from 57, heavily damaged, limped across the Channel to land at Tangmere with their wounded. Sergeant Ron Chandler, 19 year old rear-gunner of 'J-Jig', earned an immediate DFM for his action in driving off a Ju 88, despite severe leg wounds from cannon-shells. One of 630's planes managed to struggle home to base but was so damaged that it was categorised as 'beyond repair'.

The aircraft of the two squadrons were now among those equipped with 'Mandril', an airborne jamming device, designed to interfere with the enemy's radio.

The month's work had cost the Squadrons seven aircraft, though all those taking part in April's last operation, on the Aulnat airfield, near Clermont Ferrand, returned safely. Mailly-le-Camp in northern France,

BBC War Correspondent Richard North, left, interviews the crew of 630's 'E-Easy' after their de-brief on returning from the Juvisy raid *(IWM)*

'Blue' Rackley, RAAF, fourth left, and crew enjoy a smoke and chat with their ground crew before take off. *(IWM)*

Freddy Watts, centre, with his gunners. *(D. Cooper)*

housing the HQ of the 21st Panzer Division and some 15-20,000 troops was the subject of the next raid. No planes were lost when the aircraft plant at Tours was bombed twice, though Flying Officer Ron Walker of 57 had difficulty in nursing his Lancaster back to Tarrant Rushton with a badly injured rear-gunner.

When a raid on the marshalling yards at Bourg Leopold was aborted at the last minute, a 630 crew, unaware of the change of plan, circled the target area awaiting the fall of the markers and directions of the Master Bomber. There seemed an unusual absence of flak as they 'stood by' at 9,000 feet. What followed is recalled by the flight engineer, Roy Witham, in a sorty that is a classic description of a *Schragemusik* attack by a fighter equipped with upward-firing guns, a technique unsuspected by bomber crews at the time: '... without warning, a Ju 88 came up from below and tore us apart from stern to bow, killing the gunners, wireless operator and navigator. The starboard engines caught fire and I feathered them causing us to lose height rapidly. The bomb-aimer baled out. I helped the pilot as he tried to maintain height but this was impossible and he told me to move out. I released his harness and baled out at just over 1,200 feet. The aircraft exploded as my chute opened and I landed less than a quarter of a mile from the burning wreckage.'

It was about this time that the crews were issued with revolvers. These were intended as an aid to escape if shot down behind enemy lines after the invasion but caught the imagination of most of the younger members, devotees of Wyatt Earp and other Western heroes. It was as well that ammunition was limited to a dozen rounds per man, although they soon discovered that Sten gun 'ammo' was more readily, though illegally, available and fitted – more or less – the ·38 Smith & Wesson. However, being rimless, these rounds would slide out of the muzzle unless aimed 'uphill'. It was rumoured that the local wood-pigeons took to roosting on the ground until the novelty wore off!

On the night of May 19th bad weather aborted a raid on the railway yards at Amiens and led to a visit to the jettison area in the North Sea where some of the bombs had to be dropped to reduce the aircraft to a safe landing weight. Two nights later the Squadrons were over the North Sea again, this time on a mine-laying sortie that took them across Denmark to Kiel Bay. Flak and fighter opposition were heavy and each squadron lost a crew.

Mine-laying was code-named 'Gardening, mines were 'vegetables' and target areas had horticultural names, for instance, Kiel Bay was 'Forget-me-not'. RN Petty Officers would attend to the arming of the mines and an officer of Naval Intelligence was usually present at Briefing. On one occasion he told the crews that from reports received it seemed fairly certain that one of their mines had sunk a U-Boat. He added that he was happy to be able to give this information as someone had once said, of working with the Admiralty, 'It's like having an affair with an elephant; it's damned hard work, there's very little fun in it and it's seven years before you see results!

Each afternoon before a night operation, the Lancasters would be airborne on a Night Flying Test, when each system would be tested to see that all was in order. On such an 'NFT' on the 23rd a Lancaster of 57 struggled home after colliding with another from 83 Squadron, the crew of which perished when their plane crashed nearby at Revesby.

When 265 bombers from 5 Group attacked Brunswick that evening the East Kirkby crews carried a new bomb, the fearsome 'J' Type Incendiary Cluster, a 30 lb phosphorus-filled weapon. This Brunswick raid was a complete failure owing to dense cloud which cleared an hour later than forecast - an expensive miscalculation that cost the Station three crews. On the following night, however, 'a particularly good concentration was achieved' when the General Motors and Ford plants at Antwerp were bombed.

LAC Denis Howell, an electrician, recalls the day-to-day routine at the time: 'Like everyone in uniform we worked a seven day week. The only time we had off was after doing duty crew on Ops nights and our 48 hour and seven day leaves. We would usually arrive at the Flight Hut at 8 am. There, the corporal would allocate the aircraft for DI (Daily Inspection) and hand out the list of 'snags' reported by the aircrew. After giving the planes their DI we would carry out repairs and maintenance – allowing for the welcome visit of the Naafi wagon. Usually we would return to the Flight Hut after dinner and if one was lucky enough to have his three aircraft serviceable by then he would help out a mate or do necessary tasks, such as servicing the starter trolley. If there were no ops we would stand down at about 4.30 pm, apart from the Duty Crew. If ops were on, however, we would follow the armourers around the aircraft, check the wiring on the bombs and plug them in. About an hour or so before take-off the Duty Electrician would be given the 'Mickey Mouse' (Bomb Selector and Distributor) settings and would have to rush round about fifteen planes to set and check the 'Mouse'.'

The cliffs overlooking St Valery-en-Caux had been silent witnesses to the gallant stand of the 51st Highland Division during the retreat in 1940. Four years later six heavy guns stood there, facing the sea. They remained unscathed through a daylight mission by the American 8th and later attacks by other Groups. On 27th May the Squadrons were briefed to join a 5 Group bid to knock out these weapons. The Station Commander smiled as he pointed out that a 1,000 lbs bomb would fit nicely into the muzzle of one of these guns and he expected nothing but the best! For twenty minutes they pounded the pockmarked cliffs, whose massive chalk faces were lit by a ditched Lanc, burning on the water. 'Groupie' was not disappointed, for five of the guns and all of the control gear was destroyed.

A Bomber Command decision reached at this time had a most demoralising effect on the crews. It was announced that sorties to northern Europe would count as one third of an operation only. The rule was made retrospective and crews with half a tour in their log-books saw it shrink to single figures, whilst over newcomers loomed the spectre of a ninety op tour, stretching ahead, seemingly endless, except for the end some now thought inevitable. To the relief of all the rule was soon rescinded; all ops were to count in full but a tour was extended from thirty to thirty-five.

Another change implemented that summer was the transfer of the ground staff from the nominal rolls of the Squadrons to those of 55 Base and the Station. With each squadron's strength now established at over 200 aircrew it was probably intended to relieve the COs and their Adjutants of a lot of administrative work. As a result, many were disappointed to find they were no longer part of 'their' squadron, especially those NCOs and airmen who had joined 57 during the Wellington era of 1941 at Feltwell and Methwold.

The month ended with a Gardening expedition a little out of the ordinary run of things. 'Five Group News', a wall newspaper, reported: 'A long low level flight in near daylight conditions by four aircraft of 57 Squadron is worthy of note.' These four took off into the fading sun of Double BST at 23.40 hours to fly at 500 feet around the northern tip of Denmark and down the length of the Skaggerak. After planting their vegetables in the Kattegat they returned by the same route. The late sunset and early dawn were linked by the 'Midnight Sun' and for the whole seven and a half hours it was possible to see clear to the horizon. Despite this their journey was uneventful, apart from the view from two miles out of Gothenburg's neutral waterfront ablaze with neon signs, a rare sight for the crews accustomed to flying over blacked out Europe.

In all, the Squadrons carried out eleven operations during May, for the loss of five aircraft.

The beginning of June saw the start of an intensive period of work for everyone on the Station. The whole country was aware of the enormous preparations for the forthcoming invasion and throughout May the crews had seen how the increasing number of attacks on tactical targets were paving the way for this huge venture. Perhaps it came as no great surprise when all leave for ground crew was stopped until further notice.

Three operations on the first four nights of June took the crews to Saumur railway junction, a radio station at Fermes d'Urville and gun emplacements at Maisy. Ten coastal gun sites had been allocated to 5 Group in Operation *Flashlamp*, the elimination of these defences before the landings, and briefing on the evening of the 5th told the East Kirkby crews no more than was necessary for them to attack the guns at La Pernelle on the Cherbourg peninsula. Such emphasis was placed on the importance of sticking to the unusually circuitous route and of maintaining radio silence that they were pretty sure that 'D-Day' was at hand. The route had been planned to take the 'heavies' well clear of the paratroop transports and gliders and away from the warships, notoriously 'trigger happy'. Though the largest fleet ever assembled crossed the Channel that night nothing could be seen through the breaks in the cloud but an empty sea, shining in the pale moonlight. Bomber Command threw 1,136 bombers into the attacks and dropped 5,315 tons of bombs, destroying almost all of the remaining batteries along the French coast. For the East Kirkby crews the raid was uneventful, but a German news bulletin at 07.00 hours told of 'small landings which were being repulsed'. They had a laugh and went to bed well content.

A few hours sleep had to suffice. After a hurried lunch the Tannoy announced the times for Specialist and Main Briefing and soon the air was filled with the sound of Merlins running up. Haste was scarcely necessary for it was past midnight when they took off again, the targets this time, bridges near Caen where the enemy was rushing up reinforcements in the path of British troops. Difficulty was experienced in identifying the targets. No planes were lost, but a mid-upper of 57 was killed as a Ju 88 made a solitary pass at his aircraft.

The Squadrons were operating four times a week over this period and the pressure on the ground crews was pretty heavy. The bomb loads showed the change of purpose in the attacks as the 4,000 lb 'Cookies' and incendiary contain-ers of strategic bombing gave way to five-hundred pounders, eighteen to a load. On the night of the 7th the 21st Panzer Division became the objective once more when they parked their tanks in the Forêt de Cerisey en route to the Front.

In mid-June one of 630's Lancasters returned to East Kirkby, having been 'missing' since April. When Pilot Officer Watts and his crew were posted to 617 Squadron just after the Nuremburg raid they felt loath to leave a reliable aircraft behind, so they took their LE-C, named *Conquering Cleo*, with them. For ten weeks Cleo masqueraded at Woodhall Spa as AJ-Ñ (bar-Nan), taking part in a number of operations, including the radar-simulated 'invasion' on D-Day. But a service that could keep an auditor's eye on a pair of socks would not lightly overlook an aeroplane and so, her 'cover blown', *Cleo* had to leave her glamorous company and return to the bread-and-butter work of her old station.

Perhaps it was *Cleo's* unusual 'nose-art' that betrayed her, for it did not match her 'bar-Nan' code. Unlike the American Fortresses and Liberators, such art-work was quite rare on the night-bombers. The newspaper-inspired 'F for Freddie' and romantic 'P-Popsie' had been replaced with the adoption of a new convention. 'F-Fox' presented no problems but some of the codes defied illustration. A story (possibly apocryphal) ascribed to East Kirkby tells of one solution. Allegedly, the Station commander was among the little group waving the bombers off at the take-off point when 'H-How' turned onto the runway bearing a tasteful depiction of a mermaid reclining on a rock. Seeing that the rock was shaped like a large question mark, 'Groupie' chuckled, then glanced at the Padre beside him and ordered that 'How' be treated to some black paint in the morning!

Such stories brought light relief, though there was no monotony in the work, for each briefing brought variety of target, tactics, or both. An attack on the railway yards at Etampes was followed by another, apparently more successful, raid on the Caen bridges.

The tactical support role in which the bomber now flew was one of the oldest applications for military aircraft but on 12th June aerial warfare moved into a new era when the Germans launched the first V1 'Flying Bomb' on London. Though the USAAF and some RAF units had been attacking the storage and launching sites for some time, the existence of these pilotless aircraft was unknown to the public until the first dropped from the sky. Returning from a raid over France, the crews found themselves obliged to fly over the southern shires at 10,000 feet, from where they viewed the unusual sight of British light ack-ack as it 'hose-piped' at one of these missiles whose trail was marked by the pulsating orange flames from its tail-pipe.

East Kirkby was well out of range of the V1s but a side-effect was that the two RAF Regiment Flights were moved down to Hawkinge to add their Bofors guns to the barrage in Kent's 'Doodlebug Alley'. The defences were well restored when the 5 Group Anti-aircraft School moved in from

Truant Lancaster 'Conquering Cleo', ND554, LE-'C-Charlie', alias AJ-'Bar Nan'. Her code letter would be topped by a bar, indicating that 617 Squadron had two of the same letter. Other Groups used to add a small figure '2' to the code, in which case, 'Nan' would be then known as 'Nan-squared'. *Below,* P/O Freddy Watts, centre front and crew *(D. Cooper)*

Spilsby on 1st August, ostensibly to make administration easier. No reason was recorded when the school moved further afield to Strubby only weeks later.

Aunay-sur-Odon had been turned into a strongpoint by the Germans and on the night of the 14th the little Norman village was laid waste by a force of 300 Lancasters. Sledgehammer blows to destroy homes unfortunate enough to become military objectives; by morning the only structure left was the church steeple, which was soon to have a shell put through it when Canadian artillery found it concealed a sniper.

Flying in 630's 'P-Peter' that night was an ex-57 crew. When their first skipper, Pilot Officer Culliford, had been killed on his 'second pilot' sortie two months earlier they had returned to Swinderby to 'crew up' again. Now they were back, determined to make their debut together rather than tempt fate by allowing their new captain Peter Doherty to fly with strangers. 'It was', remembers the bomb-aimer, Bill Horsman, 'not a very auspicious start. We had lost our R/T and after hanging around for thirty minutes eventually bombed where other bombs were dropping. When my photo-flash went off it showed, not a village but a town. We had, in fact, joined Jerry in bombing Caen, which was still in German hands – we were not alone in being stupid!'

Arriving back at East Kirkby, they were told to make a 1½ minute tangent and rejoin the circuit. 'So we went through all the landing patter with 'Silksheen' again, landed, and taxied to our dispersal to find another Lanc on it. We asked the crew what they were doing on our dispersal and they asked why we were on their airfield! We had lost ourselves on the tangent and landed at Spilsby but they would not tell us where we were, or even the callsign. We managed to raise East Kirkby again and effect an escape. By the time we got back everyone save the debriefing team had gone to bed. We were not popular and when we confessed we'd bombed an unknown town there was talk of a Court of Enquiry – or was it a Court Martial?'

Prior to the briefing for Aunay, a signal from General Montgomery had been read to the crews, congratulating them 'on their successful attack on the two vital bridges at Caen'. Next day when Bill Horsman's photo was developed came what he calls 'the final hiccup': 'We had taken the only photo of Caen since the 5 Group attack and it showed the bridges intact!'

Another adventure with the same crew: 'Soon after take off on another trip, the hatch in the floor of the nose became detached and wedged in the aperture. By the time we got it free and back in place the navigator's maps were by the Elsan toilet in the rear ... my memories are only of incredible boobs on almost everybody's part but we did get better and became 'Breeze Boys".

A sense of humour helped. A stand-down of a few nights came as the pressure eased, and as always, the crews were not slow to let their hair down. Only at a stand-down could plans be made to celebrate a birthday or 'wet the baby's head', safe in the knowledge that ops were unlikely to interfere. Sometimes a 'binge' might lead to a bit of mischief, generally quite harmless. After all, beer was cheap and weak, spirits scarce and fairly expensive, except when the Messes got their meagre monthly allocation.

Out of camp, Boston was the nearest venue, though Skegness, despite the mines and barbed wire on most of the beach, was popular in the summer. Many a load travelled there in a little Morris Eight that bore the legend *All This and Heaven Too* (the title of a film) on the bonnet. It might well have been labelled 'unlucky', for it had three owners in as many months. Even so, the Committee of Adjustment, who dealt with the disposal of missing airmen's property seemed to find buyers for it readily enough.

Supervision of the collection of such effects was an additional duty for the Orderly Officer. Technical Adjutant Flying Officer Bill Bullock noted that he carried out this task on behalf of over 120 men during his twelve months on the Station, though his turn for duty came round but once every ten or twelve days.

LE 'P-Peter', LL966, flown by Peter Doherty and his 'Breeze Boys' *(via W. J. Taylor)*

'All This and Heaven Too' with one of her more fortunate owners, Flg Off K. Blank, right, by 'S-Sugar', LL940, mid-1944. The car has lost one of the headlight masks essential for black-out driving *(C. J. Woodrow)*

Chapter Five

The Shortest Night
June 1944

If any day on a bomber station could be called typical, 21st June 1944 started with all the promise of being so. It was bright and sunny as the aircrews had a quick wash and made a dash for the Messes to catch the tail end of breakfast. Shortly they would climb the stile and make their way through the grassy meadow to the Guardroom and on to the Squadron HQ. With lectures or a technical film show the morning would pass slowly and by noon most were making for lunch. After a quick glance through the mail rack they sought out their crew-mates and joined the queue at the hotplate. Wednesday usually produced savoury mince – only the change of menu distinguished one day from another. Conversation seemed almost forced, the atmosphere throughout the Station and, no doubt, the village as well, influenced by the fact that there had been no ops for five days, a long stand-down.

An airman pinned Battle Orders on the notice board in the lobby and a crowd gathered, craning their necks to read the names. Eighteen crews were detailed from each Squadron; Main Briefing: 20.00 hours.

By two o'clock the crews were back at the airfield, joining the usual scrum in the locker room to collect helmets, harness and 'Mae West' life-jackets before lining up at the counter of the Parachute Section, sniffing the unique aroma of canvas and mothballs. A short wait for transport and soon they were aboard the crewbus to travel around the perimeter track, the blonde Waaf driver memorising the aircraft letters shouted to her and stopping to drop crews at the appropriate dispersals.

When the crew of 57's 'A-Able' arrived at her dispersal just across the way from the old farm, they found the fitters removing the oily covers from the five foot tyres, whilst the 'rigger' polished the windscreens, one foot dangling by the forty little bombs painted on 'Able's' nose. A few minutes later the starboard inner propeller turned and 'Able' rocked as the engine fired, smoke billowing over the flattening green wheat behind. The engine was 'caught' on the throttle and the others started in succession. They were soon warmed up and the bomb doors closed as the portable generator – the 'trolley-acc' – was pulled away. A hand waved from side to side and the chocks were dragged out. Brakes off, throttles eased forward, and 'Able' moved out for her NFT.

In twenty minutes she was a thousand feet above Skegness, heading east. All systems functioned and she began a slow 180 degree turn, the acrid stench of cordite swirling forward as the guns were tested. As she lost height slowly the H2S revealed the outline of Gibraltar Point and the Wainfleet bombing range and in a few minutes 'Able' joined the circuit at Number Three. A mile away on the downwind leg Number Two had her wheels down, whilst Number One turned into the approach and lowered her flaps. 'Able' followed round and, with propellers at fine pitch, entered the funnel. Crossing the peri-track, her engines were cut and she dropped the last six feet, tyres squealing a protest in a cloud of blue smoke. In a few minutes the Lancaster was crawling into her 'pan'. With hard rudder applied, both port engines were opened up and the tailwheel described an arc on the rutted grass. 'Able' was home. Bomb doors were opened, engines cleared and switched off. The skipper broke the silence: 'It's a nice day and we're early. I think we'll have a dinghy drill. Dinghy, dinghy, prepare for ditching!' The response was not enthusiastic but, in little more than a minute, the crew were sitting in an embarrassed circle on the starboard wing, clutching various packs and ignoring the ribald remarks of passing crews: 'Don't get your bum wet!'.

Back at the billets the rest of the afternoon was idled away. The shower rooms were busy, but few bothered to shave. The NCOs of 'Able's' crew shared Hut 13 with those of a 630 crew, their third set of roommates since they arrived on 31st March the day after Nuremburg. One of these, a nineteen year old Canadian, sat on his bed, playing patience and singing the only song he ever sang: 'Mairzy Doats and Dozy Doats'. He paused to accuse his Irish fellow gunner of undue optimism for polishing the buttons of his 'best blue' in readiness for a date the next evening.

By six o'clock all had the thick, white sweaters under their battledress and a bright scarf or a silk stocking above the collarless shirt. Down the rough track paces quickened as the rural scent of the farm was replaced by the more tempting one of eggs and bacon.

The noisiest meal of the day was soon over and, flasks filled with coffee, they set off. Three lucky lads with the night off waited for the Boston bus by the padlocked phone box. They were given instructions: 'Have a pint for me'. The reply was predictable: 'Can we have your eggs if you don't come back?'

Just before eight, specialist briefing completed, the crews went into the Main Briefing Room. All eyes went to the tape marked route on the wall map. 'The bloody Ruhr!' murmured someone, but it was to the south, by the Rhine, that their objective lay.

'Flying Breakfast' - surely not the pre-flight meal with all those beans to accompany the highly-prized 'operational egg'. (Baked beans, like fountain pens, did not travel well at altitude!) *(IWM)*

A ground crew find a few moments to pose on the port inner Packard-Rolls Merlin of a Mk.I Lancaster, recognisable by the broad tips to the 'paddle-blade' propeller.

Briefing commenced: Five Group were to attack a synthetic oil plant at Wesseling, fifteen miles south of Cologne, annual output, 240,000 tons. Bombing was to be at high level and the force was to consist of 121 Lancasters, plus six Mosquitos of the Group's Pathfinder Force. Each bomb load would consist of one 4,000 lbs High Capacity bomb and sixteen 500 lbs General Purpose. Distributor setting would be 0.2 seconds to give crater spacing of 20 yards. The marking would be to the 'Newhaven' method – that is, the target would be illuminated with flares and the aiming points marked by red spot fires dropped by the Mosquitos. The chosen route should avoid some of the flak and fighter activity might well be less, Intelligence having reported that black-painted night fighters had been in action against USAAF bombers in the area that afternoon. The weather forecast followed and the party broke up.

With oleo legs and tyres compressed by their loads, the Lancs sat lower on their hardstandings as the crew buses passed. Empty bowsers were returning to the fuel dump but a last train of bombs streamed by. As each crew arrived at their plane the routine was the same. Pilot and engineer carried out their external and internal checks, the twenty pound parcels of the radar deflecting 'Window' were stowed out of the way and shortly the engines roared to join the growing chorus, flames belching from the exhausts until the throttles were drawn back to 'tickover'. Navigation lights gleamed and the tarmac was lit by a sudden glare as the landing lights dropped and rose again.

Soon warmed up, the engines were switched off while the crews had a last smoke on the dewy grass. Fifteen minutes before 'H-Hour' the gunners rose, donned their heavy suits and climbed aboard, followed by the others.

Daylight lingered on this, the longest day, but dusk was gathering quickly as DX:C-Charlie led the way round the peri track. At 23.00 hours precisely she turned onto the runway. The engines roared and the tail unit shook until the green light from the chequered caravan swept the cabin and she moved forward. Swiftly the runway swept beneath her and she approached the gap long ago torn in the boundary fence. As the wheels retracted 'Charlie' sank a little but she was flying now and a cushion of air kept her off the tarmac; she crossed the road and the Station sewage works with a hundred feet to spare.

As the lights of each bomber diminished at the far end of the field, another moved along the dotted line to await the signal. One by one they climbed away, circling to reach those high above, glinting in the last of the sun. For almost an hour they laboured upwards, for without this Radius of Action the heavily laden planes would have been over the target before reaching their operating height.

At eleven thousand feet and still climbing, they crossed the Norfolk coast, Nav lights were switched off and blackout curtains drawn tight. Below, unseen, a Royal Navy launch, RML 534, slipped her moorings at Great Yarmouth's Town Quay and cruised downstream to Gorleston and the open sea to head east.

Soon after midnight the 'Window' drop began. The rate increased as they neared the Dutch coast a little south of Overflakkee. The area never failed to live up to its quaint name and the pale orange specks could be seen sprinkling the sky ahead.

Once over land, the flak stopped and fighter flares glowed. To left and right aircraft were seen to fall in flames. Now, unusual bright lights were to be seen darting across the sky. The crews had heard of the rockets faced by the American crews by day, but this was something new to them. Constantly corkscrewing away from fighter attacks and dodging rockets the Lancasters pursued their course across Holland and Belgium, yet still burning 'planes, were to be seen.

A Ju 88, armed with conventional cannon, found 630's 'G-George' and attacked from below. The mid-upper gunner scored hits and the assailant disappeared into the clouds, on fire. The Lancaster dropped 5,000 feet before the combined efforts of the pilot and engineer managed to regain some measure of control. The engines still ran well but there was no aileron control and the rudders answered sloppily. The pilot, 'Blue' Rackley, decided to jettison the bombs and return home. Turning the aircraft round was a long, hard process, despite the combined efforts of pilot, engineer and bomb aimer and as it was completed one side of the rudder control gave way. Sheer brute force brought the rudder bar back to a central position, where it was tied with a piece of rope, though how the rope came to be there, no one knew.

At 01.00 hours the leaders turned east between Dusseldorf and Aachen on a line leading them towards Cologne, a feint intended to deceive. Fifteen miles from the city they changed course again, more southerly and aimed directly at the Union Rheinische Braunkohlen Kraftstoffen AG, now simply Target GR 1510.

The fighters landed to re-arm and refuel, leaving the field clear for the roving searchlights and the barrage of heavy flak.

With ten minutes to go, the Master Bomber found full cloud over the target. He assessed the changed situation, dismissed the Mosquitos, and ordered the 'backers-up' Lancasters to mark in 'Parramatta' fashion dropping skymarkers on the cloud as aiming points. The Main Force listened to his unhurried instructions on a reserve R/T channel, the enemy having jammed the first one with a record of 'Old Father Thames'. Then, weaving between the searchlights shining through breaks in the clouds, they went in to attack, silhouetted above the red and green markers.

As 57 Squadron's 'A-Able' closed her bomb doors, she took a slowly descending turn to the right and levelled out on a course that would take her back to the track covered on the way in, well below any stragglers heading for Wesseling. On

Room for five on a Cookie *(E. Watson)*

'If I Only Had Wings'
Ground crew in Walter Mitty mood, the pilot in a borrowed cap. The unidentified Lanc sports thirty-seven bomb symbols and the outline of a caricature figure.

Airfield view: to the left, 57 Squadron HQ. The frames on the right are stands used for working on aircraft engines. *(W. G. Wakerell)*

course, the compass had hardly settled when she was lit by a yellow glow as a rocket streaked by a few feet above and another appeared to explode underneath.

Over the Belgian border 'Able' dived violently following another explosion beneath the starboard wing but cruised steadily as she covered the last few miles to the sea. With the hostile coast just astern, there came yet another explosion below and the plane dropped again, more heavily than before. In minutes, three engines cut out. The gauges showed the tanks in use to be empty. Two hundred gallons had been lost. The main tanks still held six hundred gallons and when they were turned on the engines revived, but only for a minute. The petrol lines must have been shattered, for nothing would induce the fuel to flow and feed the three engines. The remaining engine, the port outer, ran at half speed as the engineer feathered the three propellers, jettisoned the unuseable fuel and went back to join his colleagues in crash positions for the second time in ten hours.

630 Squadron's 'G-George' crossed the coast near Ipswich, the crew preparing to bale out, for it was obvious that there was insufficient control to undertake a landing. There was a huge hole in the fuselage and the rear gunner was assisted past this. It was then discovered that his parachute

The crew of DC 'A-Able' on the afternoon before Wesseling, 21 June 1944: Johnnie Johnson M/UG, Fred Foster W/Op, Bill Martin Nav, Jack Hobbs R/G, Author Flt/Eng, 'Snow' Baker B/A. 'Snow' from New Zealand, was, at 35 the oldest aircrewman on the station. *(P. S. Baker)*

was so damaged by cannon fire as to be useless. Without hesitation, the bomb-aimer volunteered to take him on his own chute. They were tied together and dropped through the hatch but the makeshift lashings failed and the poor gunner fell to his death, the fate he had so narrowly missed when his previous crew had been killed in that tragic first take off attempt back in February.

Shaken, but safe, the bomb aimer landed, followed by the rest of the crew. Flying Officer Rackley was the last to leave, having tried in vain to set the plane on a course that would carry her clear across England before she crashed. It was not to be, for as he swung on his parachute the aircraft made ever closer circles towards him before it crashed. As he landed, his chute caught on the engine of an express train! Fortunately, the harness released, but he was quite badly injured and was picked up by the guard of a goods train.

First out and first back, 57's 'C-Charlie' called 'Silksheen', quickly followed by others. After the first dozen the rush subsided and the later planes called in at a slower rate. In the smoke-filled debriefing room the crews grabbed cups of coffee and made their reports. The general impression was that the raid had been a success, though all spoke of heavy flak over the target, persistent fighter activity, an abundance of flares, even rockets. The crews of 57's 'Peter', 'King', 'Item' and 'Baker' told of fighting off running attacks and 'Fox' claimed an Me 109. Six-thirty's stories were similar; 'X-ray' claimed a Ju 88, 'Love' had hit an Me 109. Debriefing came to a premature end.

By five o'clock the Drem system lights of the airfield were switched off and the blackout curtains of the Watch Office drawn back. The sky was empty and the Waaf at the R/T set picked up her knitting. The ambulance and fire tender were parking as Base, Station and Squadron Commanders arrived to study the blackboard on the rear wall of the office. Eleven spaces were empty in the 'Time Landed' column. The telephone rang and a moment later a 'C' was chalked in to complete the line of entries for 630's: 'G-George'.

In the Messes, the crews ate their breakfast in a babble of noise, ignoring the empty chairs. Seven dozen eggs remained unbroken. Later in the morning, ground crews with nothing to do swept and tidied the empty dispersals, while orderly room clerks prepared cables and telegrams, all beginning: 'Deeply regret to inform you that ...'.

The teleprinters at Group HQ chattered continuously as Bases reported in :

Dunholme Lodge
44 Squadron   6 Lancasters lost
619 Squadron   6 Lancasters lost

Fiskerton
49 Squadron   6 Lancasters lost

East Kirkby
57 Squadron   6 Lancasters lost
207 Squadron   7 Lancasters lost
630 Squadron   4 Lancasters lost
                 Plus one crashed

The 5 Group summary was prepared and reported to Command:

21st/22nd June '44. Wesseling Oil Plants
Detailed: 121 Lancs + 6 Mosquitos
Took Off: 120 Lancs + 6 Mosquitos
Successful: 75 Lancasters
Abortive: 8 Lancs + 6 Mosquitos
Outstanding: 1 Lanc crashed Henlow

This summary continued with a rigid adherence to accuracy in which aircraft that did not return did not count at all: '75 Lancs took off and attacked. Bombing carried out on TIs dropped blind on H2S. Explosions reported at 01.46 and 01.51. Defences: intense heavy flak, accurate for height, approx 40 searchlights. Fighters very accurate from enemy coast to target and homewards with flares, ... possibly rocket-propelled'.

Wesseling had been hit but production continued until the plant was completely destroyed the following November. Five Group had suffered its own 'Nuremburg'; thirty-six aircraft lost, equal to East Kirkby's entire effort. For the pilots of the Fw 190s with a 210 mm rocket on each wing, the short, bright night had been a Midsummer Night's Dream.

On the evening of the 22nd, 57 heard that the occupants of the dinghy spotted by Wellingtons on an Air-Sea Rescue sweep were safely aboard RML 514 as she headed for Yarmouth, and had been identified as Pilot Officer A.E. Nicklin and the crew of DX: 'A-Able'.

On the following Saturday evening, still clad in navy jumpers and bell-bottom trousers, Nick Nicklin, his navigator and engineer, walked up the track to Three Site, watching the Lancasters circling to reach the thin strips of cirrus cloud.

Leaving his companions at the officers' quarters, the engineer went on down the path to Hut 13. The doors at each end were open and as he entered the breeze rattled an empty coathanger against the curved, corrugated wall. The beds on that side of the hut were bare and the shelves above had been cleared. Nothing remained but a pack of grubby cards. No best blue with shining buttons; no more 'Mairzy Doats'.

Another new crew moved in next morning.

Chapter Six

Day and Night
July 1944

To the newcomers taking up the empty chairs in the dining rooms the Station must have seemed a bustling machine and they may have wondered if they would ever fit in. Within days they would discover that many of the crews were nearly as green as they and that squadron life was not all rush. Some of the time, they found, was for waiting and wondering.

These facts absorbed, they rapidly became accustomed to the routine. From new crews not operating on a particular night, the Duty Pilot, Engineer, and so on were chosen and these duties gave a valuable insight into the organisation and logistics of an operation.

From other duties, other lessons. One individual, having seen his name on Daily Routine Orders to be NCO i/c Beacon Party, duly reported to Flying Control late one afternoon. He left there quite bewildered, carrying a bunch of keys and a canvas bag. Help was at hand. At the MT Section he met an electrician with a cardboard box of rations and the driver of a three ton truck with a mobile beacon in tow.

Half an hour later the trailer was parked on the verge of a country road by a blue-grey caravan. The sergeant opened the bag and found two metal discs, perforated to operate the beacon in the correct sequence as it flashed the 'Letters of the Day'. He had been told the still secret letters but he was not a wireless operator and had forgotten most of the Morse Code he had laboriously swotted with the ATC. Furtively he consulted 'Lett's RAF Diary' and fitted the plates in the correct order. Meanwhile his colleagues were busy in the caravan, 'sorting out the rations' while

the kettle boiled. The tea and sugar tins were replenished and some other items were put away. At seven o'clock the truck pulled into a remote farmyard. They were welcomed into the farmhouse and the few remaining ounces of tea and sugar were handed over, along with a tin of Spam. This reappeared shortly, transformed into helpings of fried liver and new-laid eggs with new potatoes and green peas.

Soon after eight the truck parked behind a little pub and the three, with the two daughters from the farm, unpacked themselves from the cab. The sergeant exercised his prerogative and bought the drinks.

Later, as the electrician walked his girl friend and her sister home the sergeant sat on the caravan steps with the driver, eating buttered toast and surveying his command as the beacon cast its monotonous pattern across the ditches and fields.

Starlings on the van roof were a late alarm clock and the beacon was competing against the sun, higher in the sky than it should have been. There was just time for a bacon sandwich and a mug of the Carnation-rich tea before going back to camp to enjoy the day off that followed Night Duty.

Having survived three weeks, a crew would begin to consider themselves 'old hands'; in three months everyone on the Station would treat them as such. It was a landmark in a tour when a crew was detailed to play host to a 'second dickie', a new pilot, even if the presence of the extra 'bod' in the confined cabin was a nuisance.

'The Chop' came into the conversation quite frequently; death, as a word, rarely. If most of the 'planes returned safely, the memory of the one that crashed on take off, or of the rocking of the mainplanes as another blew up alongside on the run in to the target would be quickly repressed. A private Requiem Mass was held on the Station one day for some poor lad, quite unknown to most of the aircrew. To those not involved, the sight of this tragic little group of black-clad relatives seemed an intrusion. None were callous and few were hardened; it was simply that some things were best not dwelt upon. There was nothing better to concentrate the mind than the next briefing.

Crews generally flew together during training and, with luck, this would create an enduring 'family' attachment – given the losses, aquaintance with others was often transitory. Some aircrew detected hostility from Senior NCOs of the ground trades, which they put down to resentment to the rapid promotion they enjoyed, albeit often only briefly in too many cases. Indifference is probably nearer the mark. It was natural for time-serving Regulars to prefer the company of their contemporaries to that of these noisy upstarts, quite unschooled in the traditions and niceties of life in a Service Mess – those Canadians, for instance, ate bread and jam with their kippers!

On the other hand, the aircrew, long accustomed to the appelation 'Brylcreem Boys', were somewhat miffed to discover that the small allocation of this esteemed hairdressing was always put on sale in the Mess on 'Ops nights'. Thus it was grabbed in their absence by such apparently 'macho' types as the RAF Regiment.

Like other bomber stations, East Kirkby had its 'Chop Girls'. A Waaf might easliy enough make friends with one of the young airmen and, just as easily, he might be posted 'Missing'. By the time she had transferred her affections two or three times with similar results she would begin to wonder if she was now cursed with 'The Kiss of Death'. A quick posting to a nonoperational unit was the usual alternative to a nervous breakdown.

After Wesseling, Base and Squadron ground staff were kept busy introducing various 'Unit Mods' into the replacement aircraft. The aircrews carried out two raids at reduced strength without loss before the month was out.

For generations, mushrooms had been grown in the caves overlooking the River Oise at St Leu d'Esserant. Now the Germans had adapted these extensive tunnels into stores for their V-weapons and East Kirkby joined in attacks on them on the nights of 4th/5th and 7th/8th of July. On the second of these raids 630 suffered a grievous loss when their CO, Wing Commander 'Bill' Deas, failed to return, killed in action on his 69th operation. Wing Commander L.M. Blome-Jones assumed command within a few days.

Attacks were made on Calmont Chalindry and on railway yards at Nevers during the second week of July and on the 18th the Squadrons found themselves heading for Caen once more. This time, the assault on the infamous bridges and on enemy strongpoints at a nearby steel works was carried out in daylight, with greater success.

As the crews engaged on this raid landed back at Base, others were being briefed for an attack on the marshalling yards at Revigny. When one of 630's aircraft was shot down that night, only three of the crew managed to bale out. One of these, Sergeant Albert de Bruin, the midupper gunner, landed in a forest by the River Marne. For several days he lived on berries, dodging patrols from a nearby German garrison, until one night he met up with a resistance group. They were returning from a rendezvous with an aircraft that had delivered weapons to a secret landing ground. De Bruin had just 'missed the bus' and had to live with the Maquis for some months until the area was taken by US troops. He then found himself wearing GI combat kit for a week or two before eventual 'liberation'.

Though supposedly deskbound, Wing Commander Guy Gibson VC DSO DFC, leader of the dams raids, paid a short visit to the Station early in July and accompanied 57's 'B' Flight Commander, Squadron Leader Wyness, on an NFT. His appetite whetted once more, he returned on the 19th to fly with Squadron Leader Miller in 630's 'N-Nan' on a daylight raid on a site at Thiverny, thirty-five miles north-west of

Paris. His log book records that the aiming point was successful and the flak moderate. These are in fact, the last entries in this remarkable book for he was killed as he returned from another operation in the autumn.

Crews involved in an attack on Stuttgart on 21st/22nd of July reported that the fires started by 'J' Types could be seen for a hundred miles of the homeward leg.

The following night another railway target 'came in for attention'. Situated in the south of France, Givors was a key point in the communications of the area and the attack was a prelude to the Allied landings on the Riviera, planned for August. The weather that night was appalling, the bombers encountering severe electric storms when they reached France. These worsened as they flew south – one of 57's aircraft was struck by lightning and flew most of the journey on three engines. The Lancasters were found by fighters on the way out but these were shaken off, or perhaps, were scared off by the extreme conditions. The only enemy activity in the target area was a solitary gun, which fired away gamely.

In the circumstances, this lack of defence was especially fortunate for the bomber crews. Marking was delayed for sixteen minutes and the constant flashes of lightning revealed Lancasters perilously close and left the crews blinded. Over the R/T came the order 'Lights on' and for a quarter of an hour they circled the town with navigation lights gleaming.

Eventually the markers went down and the bombs followed. The aircraft turned for home and the lights were switched off. The lightning lessened but the bombers were still tossed by the violent air currents and static sparkled from gun muzzles, aerials and every other projection. The Master Bomber on that occasion, Wing Commander Ronnie Churcher DFC, recalled many years later, how he discovered on landing, that the hail had stripped a layer of plywood four inches wide from the leading edges of his Mosquito's wings.

On return, the crews were not slow to 'shoot a line' about the rare event of circling the target and bombing with nav. lights on. Whilst line-shooting in its basic form,

i.e., boasting, was quite *infra dig*, spontaneity and over-exaggeration were to be admired. Examples uncovered cannot be allowed to moulder in archives for ever: From an Australian: 'I've been in England six months; I haven't seen London yet but I've been to Berlin seven times'. A Bomb aimer's effort: 'I won't bother with a target map for Cologne. I'll use the photo I took last time!' Flak often featured in the best of them: 'When the ground crew opened the bomb doors the tarmac was littered with shrapnel!', the imaginative: 'I find that the best way to open a can of orange juice is to open a window and stick it out in the flak', or the classic: 'The flak was so thick that anyone baling out had to run along the top to find a hole to jump through!'

Soon after the bombers began regular daylight raids they were painted with squadron identity marks. At East Kirkby, these took the form of a coat of red dope on the outer surfaces of the rudders, while the fins of some bore variations of stripes, indicating squadron and flight commanders. The outlining of unit code letters in yellow to make them more conspicuous was another aid to recognition when flights were climbing to assemble into a 'gaggle', as the rather loose formations were called.

Another innovation was the introduction of 'Daylight Window', for the narrow strips dropped at night were not effective against the radar-predicted guns by day and were replaced by two inch bands, five feet long. This window made a most spectacular sight in the sunlight but the accuracy of the flak gave rise to some hairy moments for the crews, though the construction of forward airstrips in Normandy brought fighter support that generally kept the Messerschmitts at bay.

Early on the morning of the 30th the Lancasters arrived over Cahagnes, near the ruins of Aunay-sur-Odon, but the weather again took a hand. With haze below 2,000 feet, precision bombing only half a mile in front of the 2nd British Army was out of the question and the bombs were brought home.

That afternoon, a brand new Lancaster from 57 Squadron with less than two hours

Sgt 'Jock' Webster, rear right, with his 57 Sqn 'B' Flight armourers. Roy 'Lofty' Jones is on the rear left; a rather solemn Joe Craddock is right of centre *(R. Jones)*

630's 'Instrument Bashers' enjoy a smoke while seated on 1,000 pounders *(J. R. Bache)*

Background story.
Behind LE-'Fox' in this everyday
scene lies the front half of an anonymous
Lancaster *(R. D. Gale)*

flying time 'on the clock' disappeared, believed to have gone down in The Wash.

The first daylight raid on a railway target was carried out on Joigny Laroche on the last day of the month. The damage was substantial but as the crews turned away from the smoke-covered target they saw one Lancaster dropping slowly from the gaggle with an engine on fire and the crew baling out. The pilot of one of the milling Spitfire escort followed and gave a running commentary as five of the crew baled out successfully and the 'plane made a forced landing, although behind enemy lines. Not so lucky were those aboard 57's only loss that day for they were all killed, including Flight Lieutenant R.T. Clarke DFC, the popular Engineer Leader, on his thirty-first operation.

The month of July had been even busier than June and 630 lost eleven aircraft, suffering particularly heavily on the night of the Revigny raid when four crews had failed to return.

Fifty-seven's ORB sums up the month's work well: 'During the month the Squadron operated on twenty occasions; seventeen night and three daylight raids were made, in which 200 sorties were flown. Ten crews failed to return. Small tactical targets in support of our advancing armies and others against V-1 sites and storage dumps were chosen for attention. Three runs were made to Stuttgart and one to Kiel, just to 'Keep the Home Fires Burning'. ... the Squadron completing more operations in one month than has ever been completed before. For their valuable work in this achievement the ground staff are to be highly commended.'

The tremendous amount of hard work being done by the men and women supporting the bombers was certainly worthy of commendation. Aircraft had to be kept in a constant state of readiness and as daylight sorties became more frequent, some maintenance work had to be carried out at night in blackout conditions and sleep grabbed as the opportunity arose. The armourers, in particular, had a pretty rough time for a few weeks, as operations were quite often 'scrubbed' at the last minute. This usually meant that bombs, fuzed and loaded, had to be taken off. By each dispersal lay a load or two of bombs, sometimes delivered in advance, more often defuzed and left because there was no time to return them to the store. On more than one occasion a daylight raid was cancelled as the 'planes prepared to taxi out and a night operation to an entirely different type of target 'laid on'. Off would come the 500-pounders to be replaced by 1,000 lbs 'GPs', or 'Cookies' and incendiary containers. In addition, the many thousands of rounds of ammunition on each aircraft had to be changed, for the brighter 'daylight' tracer bullets would ruin a gunner's night vision if fired in the dark.

Roy Jones' recollections of the days prior to D-Day are of rumours and a more than usual sense of urgency; 'Following the news of the landings, it seemed as though we were living on the 'flights', bombing up and restocking the ammo much more often than we had been used to. For the weeks and months after we snatched sleep where and when we could. Many's the time when we were unable to get back with the others it was resourceful Joe Craddock who won something extra to supplement our rations of curled, dry cheese sandwiches and cold cocoa.'

The chill of the winter forgotten, they often suffered the other extreme now. The aircraft were finished with a paint that did not reflect light; no more did it reflect heat and after a few hours in the sun the thin metal skin became too hot to touch. The fuselage turned to a stifling oven and it was sweating toil to crank the handle of the bomb hoist and raise each bomb from the trolley to the bay.

One of the 'scrubbed' operations is worthy of specific mention. Following an NFT, the crews were told that reveille next morning was to be at 01.30 hours. Revelations followed. No.55 Base was to lead the Group which, in its turn, was to lead a massive turn out by the whole of Bomber Command. This assembly was to be surrounded by all the Fortresses and Liberators the USAAF could muster.

In the event, reveille was called at the usual time, though many were up and about after a few sleepless hours. Later in the day it was announced that the project had been abandoned and it was revealed that the destination of this huge fleet was to have been Berlin. At the last moment it was discovered that there was not enough long-range fighter cover to protect a bomber stream possibly more than sixty miles long.

'A guest drops in'
The wreckage of a Wellington lies on a 630 Squadron dispersal after a forced landing *(D. Brown)*

Chapter Seven

The Nights Draw In

August – December 1944

The yellow corn was being harvested in the fields around the airfield. There were no combine harvesters about in those days and the only engines to be heard most of the time were the familiar Merlins, running to crescendo for take off or popping and crackling as they landed, for August saw no relaxation in the 'effort'. Some crews took part in a raid on an industrial site at Siracourt, near Rouen, on the first. The raid was denied success by ten-tenths cloud but one of 57's crews was lost. Two days later the Squadrons again passed over Rouen, this time to attack a flying bomb site at Trossy St Maximin. The flak over the site was accurate and a number of the Lancs were hit, but all returned safely.

Flak was heavy again on the 5th when yet another sortie was made against St Leu d'Esserant. Cloud, and an approach well to starboard of the planned track scattered the bombing but still the caves were hit and the East Kirkby 'planes got home, perforated, but with crews intact.

A lighter episode occurred when two new pilots reported to 630's 'A' Flight Commander, Squadron Leader Millichap. 'What are your names?' he asked. 'Monk', replied one; 'Nunns', said the other. 'A Holy War!' murmured 'Millie'. 'That's all we need.'

Givors was attacked again on the 11th and late on the evening of the 12th the Lancasters took off for one of their regular attacks on Brunswick. Over 1,300 tons of bombs were dropped through cloud in fifteen minutes on this important aircraft and armament manufacturing centre.

Soon after the crews bound for Brunswick took off, those left behind found themselves being briefed for a hastily arranged attack on a road junction at Falaise. Here, the Germans suffered severe losses as they tried to escape from the trap formed as the British and Canadian Armies broke out from Caen to join up with the Americans.

Stettin was the objective when the Squadrons went on a mine-laying operation on the 16th/17th, an eight-hour round trip. Rows of flame-floats were dropped to mark the positions for the gardeners to plant their vegetables. The two Squadrons lost an aircraft each that night and two more were obliged to jettison their mines because of flak damage. Meanwhile, the city itself was receiving a battering from the Main Force and it was reported that the smoke reached over 16,000 feet. Smoke quickly covered the target when another V-1 store was attacked on the afternoon of the 18th, but the unique situation of Foret de l'Isle Adam enabled the crews to identify their objective. Flak was heavy over this island site 15 miles north of Paris and Sixty-thirty lost a crew. For the first time since the invasion enemy fighters were out in strength – some 20 to 30 Me 109s – and Wing Commander Humphreys found himself in a running battle with a particularly tenacious specimen. Two turrets were soon put out of action and with only the front guns serviceable DX 'V-Victor' was obliged to use constant 'corkscrews' and other evasions until the enemy's fuel tanks were almost dry and he was forced to retire.

Enemy warships in the harbour at Brest attracted the Group's attention on the night of 20th/21st. All the East Kirkby Lancs returned safely, though not to Base.

A couple scraped into the clifftop airfield at Predannack, on the Lizard, but the rest had to make a dash for Woodvale, near Southport, as the weather clamped down right across the country.

Now there came good news for everyone. The leave entitlement for the ground staff was restored and, for the aircrew, tour duration reverted to thirty ops.

Despite this, tours were taking longer to complete, for as squadron strength increased, crews were operating less frequently. It also made it difficult for crews to claim an aircraft as their 'own' except for the more senior pilots and even they had to be prepared to 'lend'. When one particular Lancaster was handed over to Six-thirty Squadron there was an odd reluctance among the pilots to lay claim to her. New Boy Jerry Monk jumped at the chance, then discovered the 'catch'. The new 'plane was coded 'G-George' and as no 'LE-G' had ever lasted more than a few trips the letter was looked upon as unlucky. However, Monk and his crew took the 'jinx' over and found her to be a fine aircraft, though she made an inauspicious start. All her radar and navigational aids failed on her first operation and they were obliged to 'boomerang' – make an early return.

No.5 Group made another 'double' attack, similar to that on Stettin, on 26th/27th August. The target on this occasion was Königsberg, capital of East Prussia. With the Red Army only a hundred miles away, the port was vital to the enemy.

Three nights later a second raid was made, using a new form of marking. A 'marking point' was laid by H2S and several aiming points set off from it, resulting in the destruction of nearly half of the 850 acres of dockland. Severe thunderstorms were encountered, one pilot reporting that his mount had dropped 8,000 feet before he was able to recover control. These two raids, each of 2,000 miles there and back, were not carried out without cost, for East Kirkby lost four crews.

The last of the V1s from France landed on Britain on September 2nd. Operation *Chastise*, the bombing of the launching sites and stores, had lasted three months

and Bomber Command had carried out 12,000 sorties on these targets. An Air Ministry signal to all the squadrons involved read, in part: 'The continuous and heavy bombing of the sites imposed on the enemy a prolonged and unwelcome delay in the launching of his campaign (and) effectively limited the scale of effort which he was able to make.'

The unheralded arrival of a USAAF P-51B Mustang caused some amusement one day. There was an apparent forced landing and onlookers could see the pilot evacuating his cockpit while the 'plane was still slithering along on her belly. The cause of the mishap was his erroneous belief that he was almost out of fuel and he admitted to having compounded the 'finger trouble' by forgetting to lower the undercarriage!

The Station suffered a certain degree of discomfort following an unusual 'airborne attack'. A 'rogue' barrage balloon, trailing its cable across the countryside, fouled the overhead lines carrying the power supply and again the water pumps were out of action for days.

As summer turned to autumn and the land forces continued their progress, Bomber Command was able to return to its strategic role, though now that the value of the heavy bomber as a tactical weapon had been admirably displayed it was to be called upon time and again.

The awful power of the bomber was well demonstrated when Darmstadt was attacked. Sections of the 5 Group Force bombed the industrial area from different directions and each aircraft overshot the markers by a given number of seconds. The target was devastated. The Group's bomb-carrying capacity was now so great that it usually operated alone and Bremerhaven was the next town to feel its weight. After an assault on the German Baltic Fleet in Gdynia harbour, the Dortmund – Ems Canal was bombed.

On 27th/28th of September, 630's 'D-Dog' had trouble over St Quentin on the way to Kaiserslautern. Without warning, the port inner engine caught fire. Despite the operation of the fire extinguisher system and resort to the time-honoured idea of increasing the 'revs' to blow out the flames, the fire gained hold. Flying Officer Steve Nunns ordered his crew to abandon, but for rear-gunner Jim Elliott escape was a problem for the hydraulic power to his turret was supplied by the now idle engine and he could only hope for release from outside. To his relief, his colleague from the mid-upper operated the 'Dead Man's Handle' and rotated the turret. By the time Elliott had reached the front hatch the rest of the crew had gone. His pilot's frantic gestures overcame his reluctance and he dropped into the darkness.

Steve Nunns engaged 'George', the automatic pilot and went down to the hatch. There was no one to urge *him* to jump and he looked back at the fire; surely it had abated? He returned to his seat but it was lit once more by the worsening flames, only feet away. Again he descended into the nose and again the fire seemed to diminish. This time, Nunns decided to stick with it, come what may, and he went to the chart table to plot a course for home. When he took over from 'George', the fire seemed to have gone out.

Hours later he circled East Kirkby and called 'Silksheen'. Their welcome was moderated with remarks that his load of live bombs was something they could well do without and, anyway, 'D-Dog' must be well over the permitted landing weight. Wearily, Nunns headed for the jettison zone.

On the circuit once more he was faced with the daunting task of landing a Lancaster alone. No navigator to call out the airspeed; no engineer to drop the flaps and undercarriage or to take over the throttles as he fought to correct the swing. But he put 'Dog' down and had her back in her dispersal before the rest of the crews got home from Kaiserslautern. His relief was marred by thoughts of his crew and their loved ones, especially as the bomb aimer and Jim Elliott had weddings planned for October.

He need not have worried. Jim Elliott dodged Germans, suspicious – even hostile – French farmers and swam a canal before making contact with the Maquis. They took him through the lines to Le Mans and handed him over to US troops, who took a lot of convincing as to his identity. Two days after leaving England he was back, ready to claim some sort of record. As he stepped off the Dakota he was greeted by his fellow gunner. Nor was that all; inside a week the whole crew was reunited at Base. The weddings went off as planned and in due course the crew finished their tour. Six-thirty's ORB records the event with a fine economy, both of words and fact: 'The pilot returned alone. The remainder of the crew returned the same day'(!)

By the first week of October Canadian troops had reached the Dutch island of Walcheren. Enemy forces were putting up a stiff resistance and the Squadrons joined in attacks to breach the sea wall near Westkappelle so as to flood the island.

The improved method of marking by sectors was a great success on 14th/15th when 233 of the Group's Lancasters dropped 847 tons of bombs on Brunswick, which had led a charmed life for a very long time. A further attack was made on the Walcheren dykes two nights later.

On the night of 21st/22nd of November, fifty barges were stranded when a mile of the Mittelland Canal was drained. Two more attacks were made on the Dortmund – Ems Canal in November but another sortie against the Mittelland was unsuccessful. The unusual combination of strong winds and poor visibility was aggravated by over-accurate marking, for the principal markers fell into the water and were extinguished!

When the aircraft took off on 22nd November to lay mines off Trondheim, 630's 'E-Easy' was delayed for some reason and in his efforts to catch up Flying Officer Ross Flood, RNZAF, burned up excessive fuel. Next morning, with empty tanks, he had to attempt a ditching off the Humber estuary but the aircraft hit a sandbank and was lost with all her crew.

Plots were laid in a very different direction when the Squadrons went to bomb the U-Boat pens at Bergen in Norway on the 28th/29th. Visibility became very poor, making it difficult to judge results and on return the thirty-one aircraft had to be

Flying Officer Steve Nunns, third left, with his crew and 'D-Dog'. *(J. Elliott)*
Lancasters of Six-thirty in formation. *(Mrs K. Rowland)*

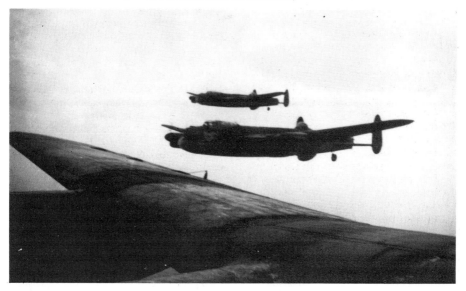

diverted to the airfield at Carnaby, Yorks, which was equipped with the fog-dispersing 'FIDO'.

Some measure of increasing Allied superiority can be seen from the losses of that period. Together, the Squadrons had lost ten aircraft in August, whereas the following three months cost but eight, two of them victims of crashes in this country. Even so, every loss was total.

Wing Commander Humphreys was captain of one of five crews of 57 Squadron to be posted out 'Tour Expired' in November, the unit's successes in this sphere totalling fourteen since August.

The Squadrons combined strength totalled forty Lancasters when they attacked Heilbron on 4th/5th of December. Fifty-seven's 'J-Jig' was lost - only the bomb aimer survived to be taken prisoner - but two of 630's suffered a damage that seemed, thankfully, rare. That flown by Flight Lieutenant Frank Jones was struck by a number of incendiary bombs and some were found embedded in the wing on his return, whereas Flight Lieutenant Baugh, pilot of another, received an injury to his hand when one of these missiles came through the cabin roof. The Squadron was not so fortunate a few days later when attacking the Heimbach Urftdam for they lost an aircraft in a tragic collision over the target.

Among their pilots taking off for Munich

Flt Lt Hazen H. Long DFC, RCAF, flew the last nineteen ops of his tour in LE-'F-Fox', LM259; she was lost in December 1944. *Above* 'Fox' shows off her 630 'A' Flight Leader's stripes. In the background, another Lancaster is 'running up' as her bomb doors close. *Opposite,* in close-up, the bomb symbols were usually red or green, the lighter ones, probably yellow, indicate daylight sorties. *(Both R. D. Gale)*

ten days later was Les Barnes. It was ten months since he had left for Stuttgart and his perambulations had taken him over the Pyrenees into Spain and, eventually, to Gibraltar. On his return to East Kirkby there were no aircrew left who could remember him but the Squadron had not forgotten him, nor the small matter of some twenty-six ops he 'owed' them to complete his tour. Back pay had to be earned.

The winter soon began to make itself felt, particularly with the discomforts of the poorly heated huts, so prone to condensation. On the other hand, the inclement weather reduced the amount of flying and gave a little more free time. The Station cinema was always well patronised and there were facilities for many sports and pastimes. For those who wanted to escape for an hour or two there were simple pleasures to be found. A 'Toc

H' Canteen established in the village hall was popular. It was 'manned' by local ladies, assisted by other volunteers. One of these was Flying Officer Courtenay Grebby who was also involved in the organisation of Bible Classes and discussion groups in what was known as the Fireside Fellowship at the Methodist Chapel. Many found pleasure and company at these venues and the pennies they paid for their cups of tea accumulated into a considerable sum which went to help provide similar comfort for the Forces serving abroad. Many a Saturday night the little hall at Old Bolingbroke, known as 'The Sweat Box', bulged with airmen, Waafs and Land Army girls, jiving until the last waltz and 'The King'.

Some of the ground crew bred rabbits as a hobby, and a profitable one, for wholesome meat found a ready market in rationed Britain, while a couple of others kept ferrets with which they cleared the pests from the fields. The ferrets worked with the blessing of the farmers, unlike, apparently, a Chaplain who was hauled before the local 'Beaks' and fined five shillings (25p) for poaching!

A cycle ride to one of the local pubs was always a popular way to spend an evening,

at least during the first week after the fortnightly pay parade. At a pub in Stickney, an elderly local resident insisted on playing the piano every evening. As he used only two fingers his efforts were not popular and aircrew with slightly jagged nerves managed to feed him some of the 'Wakey-Wakey' pills they were issued with. Thus reinforced, he played on and on – and on, presumably staying awake all night. He 'got the message' and retired. There was a larger Red Lion along the road at Revesby, sometimes with a pianist for entertainment, but always with a warm fire to sit and yarn by in the winter. It also had an advantage over the Station's 'local' in that it had a seven day licence and could open on Sundays.

East Kirkby's Red Lion was the nearest common ground where aircrew and their supporting staff could meet. In addition to his butcher's shop, landlord Walter Handson also worked the 1½ acre smallholding that went with the house. Hired help was unavailable but he was granted the services of a German prisoner-of-war. As Christmas approached, the War Department told the Handsons that they would like to close the POW Camp for the short holiday. Could they find their prisoner a

bed? They agreed, but Iris Handson reasoned in her kindly way that it would not seem right at Christmas for everyone to have presents to open while nineteen year old Helmut had none. Her husband asked him what he would like. Helmut said that his greatest wish was for a pair of shoes. He had not possessed shoes since he was a small boy; first the Hitler Youth, then the Wehrmacht, always boots.

Walter did not begrudge the cost for Helmut was a good worker; clothing coupons were the problem. A couple of elderly customers agreed to provide these on consideration of two halves of mild and Helmut was able to put the shadow of the jackboot behind him.

Enjoying his short spell of freedom, Helmut stood in a corner of the passage one evening whilst a crew were having a 'binge' in the 'public'. Seeing this lonely figure, the skipper asked Mrs Handson – always 'Mabel' to 'the boys' – who he was. She explained. 'Can't he come in ?' they asked. Mabel said that she didn't mind, but they were in the RAF and he was a German. 'The poor b------ can't help that!' was the response, and Helmut found himself enjoying the party, which was in celebration of the end of a successful tour of ops over the Fatherland!

One night shortly before this, the same crew, lingering over a last pint, listened sympathetically as Mabel complained of the housewife's Christmas dilemma, then, as now, so much to do so little time. She had not had a moment to decorate the parlour so the gallant lads offered to help. The paper chains that had had to serve from year to year looked a little unhappy but new ones and such things as balloons were quite unobtainable. However, by the time Mabel had finished polishing the beer glasses the job was done and she was most impressed, though she noticed that the 'balloons' were all of the same pallid colour.

Walter was still working in his shop, trying to provide his customers with some sort of Christmas dinner and she called him to see the airmen's handiwork. Only after the tears of laughter had subsided was he able to take his wife to one side and explain a little more of the facts of life,

contraception being his main theme! 'Well', confessed Mabel, 'I didn't know what such things looked like.'

For other crews on the station, Christmas that year was less festive. Many returned from a raid on Gdynia on 18th December to find the airfield fogbound and had to spend a week away from Base, without even the luxury of a razor. Jerry Monk landed 630's 'G-George' on the huge emergency runway at Woodbridge in Suffolk. 'The weather clamped down for days' he recalls, 'and eventually we tried to fly home. We got as far as Swinderby and had to land there, finishing the journey by lorry. Arriving at about seven o'clock on Christmas night, I was so worn out I went straight to bed.'

'My abstemious night meant that I was the first one down at the Flight Offices in the morning. The phone rang; there was a war on. The two aircraft were required from each Squadron. I 'put myself on' and got my crew de-icing 'N-Nan'. Before they took off, Wireless Operator Joe Baldwin received news that his mother's home had been hit by a flying bomb. He was granted compassionate leave to go home, his place being taken by Reg Fletcher, of Steve Nunns' crew. Jerry Monk continues: 'Eventually the Intelligence Officer turned up and told us the target was St Vith and we could make our own arrangements. I picked a bombing height of 14,000 feet and flew straight to the target – tank concentrations in the Ardennes battle. We made our run over the battlefield in brilliant sunshine to find all the Halifaxes Command possessed crossing at a tangent, about six thousand feet above. Thousand pounders and Window fell around us like tinsel but all the bombs missed us. This time we were diverted to St Eval in Cornwall.'

Reg Fletcher remembers the raid well and subsequent events even better. He had also spent Christmas at Woodbridge and though the magnificent runway was a welcome sight to crews in trouble, domestic facilities were poor. St Eval, they found was even worse, for the 'locals' treated the intrusive 'bomber boys' as pariahs and made them less than welcome. Thus, when the weather cleared up north two days later they were glad to escape. Like Predannack, St Eval had a cliff-top runway which made a Lancaster take off a rare experience, for it would be scarcely airborne before it fell over the end. The gunners were able to gaze back up at the 200 foot granite cliffs, which took their minds off worry of what might lie ahead.

Safely aloft, Jerry turned back and beat up the airfield, finishing with a low run

Flt Lt 'Jock' Hoare, RAAF, in the cockpit of LE 'L-Love', NN774. The projection near the 'bomb tally' is the port aerial for 'Rebecca', a navigational aid. *(D. Brown)*

past Flying Control. As they passed, all the crew gave their opinion of 'St Evil' with V-signs of a strictly non-Churchillian variety. Unfortunately, the telephone is faster than the Lanc and Jerry found himself on the CO's carpet when he got back to Base.

Visibility was still poor on the 30th and the airfield lights were switched on at midday in an attempt to provide a safe haven for a USAAF B-17 in distress. Station records have it that the aircraft, which had limped across the North Sea after a raid and was unable to reach its Bedfordshire base, crashed on the runway, but local memories are quite clear in that it crashed on the hill with the loss of all crew.

Above upper: **Tour expired, Flt Lt A.E.Nicklin DFC, fourth left, and crew and their ground crew with their second 'A-Able' LM624, which replaced the ditched ND471 and** *lower* **LM624 with 'daylight style' code letters and tail markings indicating a Flight leader** *(both P.S.Baker)*

Opposite
'OH 'U' BEAUTY!'
When Flt Lt E.Harris, RNZAF, and his crew were allotted LE-'U-Uncle' NG123, in September 1944, their first act was to commission some splendid art-work. Through the winter of '44-'45 'U-Beauty' became a photogenic favourite. *Top left,* **Instrument Mechanics, Corporals Bache and Bonser with 'U'; Six-thirty's No.1 Hangar is in the background** *(J.R.Bache). Top right and centre,* **show 'U' without the Bomb Tally, and** *lower left* **the driver of 630's crew bus, a Bedford QL truck and** *lower right* **with the crew** *(all T.R.Lockett)*

52

Chapter Eight

The Year of Victory
1945

The fog lifted with dawn on New Year's Day and the Squadrons took off for a daylight raid on the Dortmund-Ems Canal, following this with an eight aircraft sortie on the Mittelland, where once again, the banks were breached and a considerable length drained. All returned safely from these raids, though many Allied aircraft were destroyed on Continental airfields as the Luftwaffe made its contribution to the Ardennes counter-offensive. German troops taking part in the advance were the target when 57 and 630 joined an assault on Houffalize on 6th January.

Munich received another blow from the 5 Group fist the following night. The pounding of the synthetic oil plants was beginning to pay off. Although the area to be defended was now much reduced, enemy pilots often found themselves grounded through lack of fuel and the East Kirkby crews were able to make the long run to Bavaria without loss on this occasion.

Returning from her sixteenth operation with her regulars, Monk and Co, 630's 'G-George' had been diverted yet again. They arrived back at Base as the crews were being briefed for Munich and the Squadron Commander decided that another crew should take 'George'. Jerry Monk recalls the event: 'Short of a bomb aimer, mine, Len Knowles, was detailed to fly with them, with George 'Billy' Billings as skipper. They lost an engine immediately after take off and, after jettisoning into the sea, aborted to Base. At the point of touchdown, the Lanc bounced. As the engines were opened up, the other engine on the same side cut out, the wing touched the runway and she cartwheeled into the ground. My bomb aimer survived after

lengthy hospitalisation but several of the crew were killed. Billy was found many yards away, still strapped in his (my) seat. He lost an arm. We have met many times since and he makes light of it all. 'G for George' had lived up to her reputation and 630 never had another'.

From January 17th, deep snow lay across Lincolnshire and indeed over the rest of Europe, curtailing operations for weeks. The traditional chore of clearing the runways and perimeter track kept everyone busy, for only police and cooks were excused. For some of 630's pilots this job must have been something of a novelty, for at this time four of them wore the khaki of the South African Air Force.

Jim Garraway cannot have been too pleased when he found himself posted to serve as Detail Corporal at East Kirkby's MT Section, for he had to leave his wife at Swinderby. The friendship which led to their marriage had begun in somewhat 'bittersweet' circumstances for to Jim fell the duty of driving the 'artic' truck which served as a hearse when Service funerals were held at the village church at Norton Disney, while the pretty LACW Jean Wakeham drove the car that carried the padre. Now, close to their first anniversary, a transfer had been 'wangled' for Jean and her dog 'Mickey'.

Swinderby had been built as a 'peace-time' aerodrome with (mostly) permanent accommodation and East Kirkby must have been a shock to Jean Garraway when she arrived, laden down with kit-bag, small kit, gas mask and tin hat: 'It looked like a concentration camp to me in the dusk of a winter's day. Everywhere was knee deep in snow and slush and the 'bods' were dressed in a variety of gear to keep them warm. All the pipes were frozen at the WAAF Site. A slight dignity was preserved by the erection of a hessian screen along a ditch after days of degradation – and it wasn't just our marrow that was frozen!

'Each morning, Jim (Ginger to the lads) would send my dog to the Waafery to fetch me. He knew my hut and bed; the first I knew was when my blankets hit the floor. Fortunately we girls could use the Corporals' Mess and I was able to have meals with Jim. The WAAF were also provided with fresh milk which was a great treat. The mess was decorated most beautifully inside, for an unknown artist had painted the panels with various murals such as 'Ave Maria' and 'Swan Lake'.

'We had great fun at times and there was excitement when the Entertainments Officer acquired some old cinema seats and equipment and the mess was extended so we could have film shows. A 'spooky' film was being shown one night and a scarred face appeared on the screen. The heroine screamed, Mickey barked, Waafs yelled and the 'erks' collapsed in hysterics, turning drama into farce.'

Drama was real enough for Jean, one night. She was often detailed to take Operations Reports to 5 Group HQ at Morton Hall, the other side of Lincoln: 'Being an important assignment, there could be no stopping for anything or anyone. It was a cold and lonely journey in the blackout with only slit headlights. There was no heating in vehicles in those days and the side windows were often missing. On one of these journeys I was terrified as someone leapt from a dyke bank onto the van

PD317, the last of Six-thirty's ill-fated 'G-Georges' *(E. Watson)*

Dispensing 'Window' was the flight engineer's chore. So too was unloading it, usually accomplished by throwing the packages up into the escape hatch under the nose. Ted Watson pauses here while preparing for the raid on Positz, 13 January 1945, when he flew in LE-U with Pilot Officer McGuffies *(E. Watson)*

Jerry Monk, centre, and some of his crew, Christmas 1944 *(E. Watson)*

'Bob and Bobby'
Best blue and borrowed dress.
(Mrs J. Garraway)

and hung on. I 'put my foot down', but in vain, for the engine was 'governed' to conserve fuel. My heart was thumping but Mickey sized up the situation and went for the chap's throat and he let go.'

The hard frosts of January eased a little in February and with the slight thaw came the inevitable burst pipes – some five hundred were reported, in addition to damaged tanks, boilers and cisterns.

The bombing continued as the weather improved, invariably on German targets now; the lifelines of communication of the Dortmund-Ems and Mittelland Canals being attacked as soon as repairs appeared complete. On February 13th the Squadrons took off once more, their target, Dresden. The 57 Squadron diarist noted: 'This was the first attack by Bomber Command on Dresden'. Six-thirty's records refer to the city as 'a virgin target' but few bomber crews could have viewed any part of Nazi Germany as a damsel in distress or concerned themselves with fine china. Nearer to their hearts were the thousands killed in other air raids on such places as Coventry and Plymouth. Seventy-one rockets fell without warning on London and the south east that very week. If Dresden had not been chosen, no doubt the latter-day critics and the 'experts' armed with splendid hindsight would have searched elsewhere for a stick with which to belabour those who had advocated, or even condoned, aerial bombardment – ignorant of, or ignoring, the fact that most British people were glad to be numbered among them, for it was Hitler and Goering who had sown the wind.

March started with tragedy on the doorstep when a Lancaster from 57 engaged on a fighter affiliation exercise, collided with another from 207 Squadron. The latter survived to make a safe landing back at Spilsby but 57's crew were killed as their stricken aircraft fell at Ruskington Fen and with them died an aircrew cadet who had 'gone along for the ride'.

Threats of enemy invasion were now a thing of the past and much of the barbed wire and other defences were being removed. In early March it was ordered that the anti-aircraft guns were to be dismantled and kept in the Armoury in a state of readiness. Intruder attacks, particularly at dusk and dawn, were becoming very frequent and the wisdom of this decision was soon to be called into question. At 01.45 hours on the 4th, just after four Lancasters had landed from a raid on Ladburgen, a Junkers Ju 88 joined the circuit. 'Scram' action was effective and the airfield lights were switched off. Denied a victim in the air, the Bandit turned his attention to targets on the ground. The MT Section was raked with cannon and machine gun fire and, in the 'follow-through' as the attacker swept over, the salvo reached 57's Briefing Room. Five of the debriefing team were severely wounded, including Squadron

Officer B.B. Hayward, the WAAF CO, and Flying Officer A. Healey, the Signals Analysis Officer, who subsequently died of his wounds.

Belatedly, it was ordered that twin Browning machine guns were to be mounted in all displacements and these were to be manned on receipt of a Red Alert.

There were no casualties in the MT Section, though ten vehicles were damaged. By this time, the Garraways were 'living out' in East Keal. 'We cycled each way,' recalls Jean, 'sometimes passing each other, according to duties (just stopping for a quick kiss). It was on one of these fleeting meetings that I learned of the Ju 88 attack. There was quite a family atmosphere in the Section. LACWs 'Casey' English and 'Dusty' Burrows also lived out, with their sergeant husbands. When 'Bobby' Henman (how fond they were of nicknames!) married Corporal Bob Copeman she was able to look the part in a wedding gown loaned by the wife of the MT Officer.'

One of Jean Garraway's more bizarre memories of those days: 'It seemed that

'Happy Family'
Some of the MT Section. Corporal Jim Garraway is at the front.
(Mrs J. Garraway)

every household in East Keal kept a pig and when the time was right the slaughter-man came along. When cycling home one evening I could hardly believe my eyes to see disembowelled pigs hanging on every garden hedge.'

Fifty-seven Squadron lost a crew on a raid on Harburg on March 7th/8th and another on the 20th/21st, though this, the loss of LM653 over Bohlen was the unit's last operational loss of the war. That particular night was ill-fated from the start for another of their Lancasters crashed shortly after taking off, hitting a house between Stickney and Stickford, killing five of the crew.

A crash on take off did not always result in an explosion, though this was often due only to quick work by the fire tender crew. If only one or two of the bombs went off the result was a violent affair and mangled metal was thrown far and wide. One can imagine the terror struck into the prisoner as he lay on his bed in a cell of the Nissen hut Guardroom when an oleo leg from a Lancaster undercarriage tore through the fragile roof of his gaol. Next morning, on his routine visit, the Padre gazed at the missile, weighing a hundredweight or more, and at the poor 'jankers-wallah'

whom death had missed by inches. 'Remember', he observed, 'the wrath of the Lord will seek out the wrongdoer, wheresoever he may hide!' Mercy was to prevail later and the miscreant was let off.

The Squadrons were out in strength on 23rd March when thirty six of their crews joined in a 'softening-up' attack as the 21st British Army Group faced its last obstacle, the crossing of the Lower Rhine at Wesel. Operation *Varsity* was expected to be a costly operation but in the event bombardment from the air enabled the troops, waiting only seven hundred yards away across the river, to make the crossing with minimal casualties. General Montgomery's

Above: **View of the MT section, left, from entrance road of Technical Site.**

Below: **Christmas decorations in the more sparsely populated Sgts' Mess, 1945** *(both L. G. Wakerell)*

message to Bomber Command next day read: 'My grateful appreciation for the quite magnificient co-operation you have given us in the Battle of the Rhine. The bombing of Wesel last night was a masterpiece and was the decisive factor, making possible our entry into the town before midnight.'

A special event in March for 630 Squadron was the award by HM The King of the Squadron Badge and Motto. The Badge was, most appropriately, the Lancaster Rose, indicative of the only aircraft type the Squadron ever flew, and the Motto: 'Nocturna Mors' – 'Death by Night'.

The Squadron continued to suffer casualties during the last weeks of operations for one of their aircraft crashed in April and when two failed to return out of eleven sent to bomb Leipzig on the 10th/11th of the month it was a loss rate too reminiscent of the bad nights a year before.

Chance took Flight Lieutenant John Chatterton 'home' to serve as 630's 'Check Pilot' after a tour with 44 Squadron and a stint of instructing at Syerston. 'I was born in the middle of the airfield!' was a certain conversation stopper whenever he used it in the Mess and he could be sure of ribald remarks about there being a shortage of gooseberry bushes or of the stork being given the wrong QDM (compass heading). John had, indeed, been born at Hagnaby Grange and as a five year old had made his way to school over the fields now crisscrossed with concrete.

But what was left of the old family home did not survive the war. The farm had been a bone of contention from the day the Station opened, generating paper at an alarming rate. Within days of his arrival the Station Commander had paid a visit and seen for himself the state the house was in. Flying Control suggested it be pulled down, claiming the 45 foot poplar trees were of no use as camouflage but were a hazard to aircraft. Furthermore, they blocked the field of fire of the AA guns. OC RAF Regiment disagreed, saying that the trees presented no problem to his guns and the house would make a nice billet for his lads. 'Cost too much to repair the damage caused by the contractors, I'm afraid', said the Group

Captain. The Works Office's response was firm: 'The RAF did the damage'. 'All done before we came'. said the CO. 'Works and Bricks' played their trump card: 'We know where you acquired the wood to build a stage in the Dining Hall!' The CO admitted to allowing this as the wood was already torn out and he assumed demolition had begun. Anyway, they hadn't used very much.

In March, 1944, Flying Control complained again. The farm was still a hazard owing to its proximity to a runway, and it blocked their view of five dispersals and half a mile of perimeter track. The Station Commander wrote to Group, requesting permission to clear the site. Everyone else wrote to Group. Air Commodores passed minutes to each other and a stern reply was composed: 'Stop this nonsense', it said in effect. 'If Command get wind of what's happened to requisitioned property there will be trouble'.

Fate took a hand on 17th of April, 1945, and settled the matter. The bombers were being prepared for a raid on targets near Cham, on the Czech border. By 17.45, bombing-up was nearly complete but trollies were still being moved under PB360, Fifty-seven's 'U-Uncle', when fire broke out. Theories have been advanced as to the cause; whether from a flooded carburettor or from the premature detonation of a photoflash, – the results were horrendous. The Station fire tender arrived and caught the full blast as two one-thousand pounders exploded. A fire-

man was killed, along with a soldier of the Pioneer Corps. (The Pioneeers' job was the everyday maintenance of the airfield but enthusiasm drew them to lend a hand at bombing-up and other tasks when they had a spare moment). Despite his injuries,

The badge of 630 Squadron. The Red Rose of Lancaster and the motto translates as 'Death by Night'.

LAC Silkstone and his Dodge oxygen truck. Of such robust construction are the 'Ground Cyclinders' seen here that thousands, of wartime origin are still in use with the RAF even now *(J.R. Bache)*

fireman, LAC William Thaxton carried his wounded corporal to safety. Others too, ignored the danger of further explosions in their rescue attempts.

Warned of the incident, the Station Fire Officer, Flying Officer Grebby, left his tea and rushed to the airfield. As he pulled up in his jeep outside the Guardroom for information, there was a mighty explosion and he hurried towards the black smoke that hung over Hagnaby Grange. He arrived to find that two more men, an ambulance attendant and another airman, had been killed and more injured. He joined Flying Officer John Gott in the rescue work, as did others, notably Corporal Raymond Forster of PB360's ground crew, Corporal Leslie Friswell and LAC Frederick Brown, all of whom had been injured.

By now three aircraft were ablaze and the bombs on these began to explode. Number Three Hangar nearby was being used as a store for incendiary bombs and Armaments Officer Flight Lieutenant John MacBean saw that boxes containing these were alight. With an extinguisher, he ran down the aisle between the stacks of bombs and had almost reached the far end where the fire had started when another blast hurled him back, fortunately blowing out the flames at the same time.

Flying Officers Gott and Grebby set about putting out minor fires of dreadful potential, such as the blazing tyres of loaded bomb trollies, for, in the latter's own words, 'I thought someone ought to do something'. He next approached a burning aircraft, intending to remove a body that lay close by, despite warnings that a 4,000 pounder lay in the flames. At that moment there came a further explosion and he sustained a deep wound in the thigh – his life was saved only by the speedy application of a tourniquet made from the Station Commander's braces. Yet, as he was being carried away, he had to be assured that he was not depriving a worthier case of a stretcher.

Tom Raines 'had his knees under the table' at Magor Farm, just a few hundred yards from the 57 dispersals where he worked as a fitter and, his duties finished for the day, had joined the Traves family for tea. Suddenly, the house shook and a barometer fell from the wall, showering Mary, the daughter of the house, with glass and mercury. Her father, with a flash of wartime humour, remarked: 'I see the glass is falling; we're in for a storm!'

Flying Officer Courtney Grebby, the Station Fire Officer *(J. Monk)*

The dispersal where the fire which led to the tragic explosions began, showing the proximity to Hagnaby Grange farmhouse, right. The photograph dates about a year earlier and the 'N-Nan' shown refuelling is ND560, a Mk.III Lancaster lost in the summer of 1944. *(Imperial War Museum CH12868)*

Further ominous rumbles prompted them to take a more serious view of the situation and they lay on the floor for a time before deciding to leave the farm. As they set off to make their way along the hedgerows away from the clouds of smoke over the airfield they saw that new bed linen, spread on the grass to bleach in the sun, was now pinned down and scorched by shrapnel.

Ambulances and medical teams were now arriving from Spilsby and Coningsby to help with the casualties, of which fourteen, including some civilians, were serious.

Dennis Howell was setting the 'Mickey Mouse' again that evening and recalls: 'Suddenly the whole Squadron seemed to blow up. I helped tow some 'planes away before we were told that the aerodrome was to be evacuated'. Six-thirty's aircraft were abandoned where they stood, for a fourth Lancaster was now on fire and it appeared a losing battle. Though the frequency of explosions lessened eventually, the 500 and 1,000 pound bombs loaded that afternoon had been fuzed with half and one hour delay pistols and there remained the danger of further sympathetic detonations, made worse by the loads of bombs taken off when a previously planned operation had been 'scrubbed', for these were now scattered at random. Through the night East Kirkby, Station and village alike, waited, but as the sporadic crackle of .303 ammunition died down, a silence the fields had not known for a long time settled in.

Next day, the far side of the airfield looked like a battleground. Six aircraft had been totally destroyed and fourteen others had varying degrees of damage. The tiles from the roof of Hagnaby Grange were strewn among the trees and all around live bombs lay like sleeping tigers among the mangled aluminium and the massive pieces of masonry torn from the dispersals.

When Jim Garraway turned up for work that morning, he and three other NCOs were somewhat disconcerted when the MT Officer handed them large envelopes to contain their personal possessions, and a sheet of paper for a 'Last Letter' – 'just in

case'. One by one they were sent out with lorries loaded with sandbags and manned by Pioneers and four prisoners released from the Guardroom for the 'occasion'. They were to pile the bags around each bomb to contain the blast, if.... . This work was accomplished without incident, though a squad of airmen, set to filling some of the holes in the peri track, came to a crater with bombs in the bottom. They sent for a crane and retired to 'brew up' while they waited. The Coles crane arrived as the kettle boiled, then followed a mighty blast which considerably enlarged the crater. Tea never tasted better. Meanwhile, Jim Garraway, having dived for cover behind a blast wall, found himself face to face with an old school chum he had not seen for years. It was here that one of the Pioneers was heard to murmur: 'If I'd known it was going to be dangerous I wouldn't have bloody well come'.

Gingerly, the armourers approached each bomb to examine the fuze for the tell-tale stains that would indicate that the seconds were elapsing. Eventually, all the weapons were made safe, and everyone, not least the armourers, could breathe again.

There were countless acts of gallantry throughout the incident and at least a few of them were recognised later with the award of the MBE to Flight Lieutenant MacBean, Flying Officer Gott GM and Flying Officer Grebby, whilst to Corporals Forster and Friswell and LACs Brown and Thaxton went British Empire Medals.

It was looked on as a matter of pride as well as being a primary duty that an airfield and its aircraft should be operational at all times and it was a sad situation for the Station, with its people killed and injured, virtually all the 'planes of one squadron lost and the other grounded.

Responsibility for getting the airfield back into action fell on the Works Office, who were quick to respond. There was a very large hole and a number of smaller ones in the track and four hardstandings had been destroyed. The doors at each end of the hangar and much of the sheeting had been torn off. Three dispersal huts had vanished.

The airfield was partially useable by

Flt Lt J. Hoare, RAAF, and crew of 630 Squadron, Spring '45. *(Mrs K. Rowland)*

25th April and five crews from each Squadron were briefed for a daylight operation much to their liking. They were to bomb the SS Barracks at Berchtesgaden and, close by, the opulent homes of Goering and Bormann. Surrounding mountains made the 'Eagle's Nest' difficult to hit but the crews came home safely and must have felt that they had shaped history.

That night the Squadrons sent four 'planes apiece to lay mines in the 'Onions' area – Oslo Fjord. This turned out to be the Station's last offensive operation and Flying Officer Jacobs (630), landing at 02.53 and Flying Officer Meeks of 57, six minutes later, were the last to land.

Five Group's final raid, an attack on Kiel, took place later on the 26th and then, suddenly, there were no targets left. Bomber Command had played its role in the victory to the full. Field Marshal von Rundstedt recorded soon after: 'Air power was the decisive factor in Germany's defeat. Lack of petrol (due to bombing) was the second and the destruction of the railways the third. The other principal factor was the smashing of the home industrial areas by bombing.'

With the Continent in chaos the end could not be far away, but while fighting continued in Germany the crews were glad of the opportunity to join in Operation *Exodus*, the repatriation of thousands of Allied prisoners-of-war.

On 'VE Day', May 8th, the Station paraded at 14.30 hours to hear the Prime Minister's broadcast relayed over the Tannoy system. Preparations had been made in advance for the celebration dance that was held that evening. It is still remembered in the village as 'quite a party'.

Not everyone had the day off, for *Exodus* continued and a dozen 24-man loads were carried from Brussels to Wing in Buckinghamshire. Such satisfying work was celebration enough. Among the East Kirkby pilots that day was Flight Lieutenant Michael Beetham DFC, whose first arrival had been a dramatic one. A year earlier he had been pilot of the ill-fated 50 Squadron aircraft and had emerged through the cloud on his parachute to see her in flames below. None of his happy passengers on VE Day could have imagined that the man in the front seat was destined to become Chief of Air Staff some thirty-five years later.

By the end of May the two Squadrons had brought more than 1,800 ex-prisoners home. One, a gunner with 57, raised a laugh when he told of the interrogation that followed his capture. The Luftwaffe captain studied his brief which told him the aircraft code letters taken from the wreckage, then offered a cigarette. 'Fifty-seven, eh?' he smiled. 'How's Taafe?' The question was intended to disarm but had the opposite effect. This mere sergeant had never heard 'Groupie' referred to by his surname. As he heard it, the Germans even knew the nickname of the Welsh fitter who worked on his aircraft. He was speechless!

Like other units, 57 and 630 were able to give at least some of their ground staff a glimpse of the results of their work by taking them on 'Cook's Tours' over Cologne and the Ruhr. Three of 57's Lancs also took part in Operation *Spasm*, flying a few 'VIPs' and some of the Senior NCOs to Berlin for an overnight stay. The bomb trollies were still trundling round the perimeter track, for some of the crews were employed on Bomb Disposal Flights, when various bombs, especially incendiaries, deemed unsuitable or unsafe to keep were dropped in jettison areas. Six-thirty's 'R-Robert' was engaged on such a flight on 15th June. She reported by radio that her bombs had been dropped but no more was heard and she failed to return. Both Squadrons joined in the search but no clue was found to account for the Squadron's last aircraft loss.

Soon after this tragedy news came through that 630 were to move to Skellingthorpe but nothing came of this and as the last remaining Australian and Canadian members were posted out to holding units in readiness for their return home, it soon became obvious that Six-thirty would not be going to 'Skelly' or anywhere else.

The Squadron's Briefing Room performed its last function as the setting for a farewell dance on July 17th. The next day the Unit paraded before its Commanding Officer and was stood down. In just twenty months No.630 Squadron had earned itself a niche in the history of Bomber Command and of the Royal Air Force. From formation to the end of the European War it had been in continuous action, a total of 2,453 sorties, including all the sixteen raids of the Battle of Berlin. As well as the many tons of mines laid in enemy waters, 10,347 tons of bombs had been dropped though at the cost of seventy Lancasters. More than seventy members had been decorated for their services.

Within a few days the Squadron's aircraft had been flown out and all that remained of 'Six-thirty' were memories – and they remained still.

Flight engineer A. H. Ricketts and navigator Ray Haslam flew LM653 DX-'Q-Queen' for most of their tour but the aircraft was lost towards the end of the war with another crew.
(A. H.-Ricketts)

Above: The Intelligence Library where classified information was available to the crews. *Below:* Bob Hamilton, second left, and crew with Section Officer Kay Seward prior to a 'Cook's Tour' of bomb damaged areas of Germany. *(both Mrs K. Rowland)*

Chapter Nine

Peacetime Again

Europe was free – of the Nazis, at any rate, – but a bitter war raged on in the Far East and No.57 Squadron was one of ten ordered to begin training as part of the Long Range Bomber Group that was to augment the bomber offensive being mounted against Japan. 'Tiger Force', as it was known, was to go east in early November and a convoy was already being assembled at Panama to transport the engineer battalions that were to prepare airfields on islands still in enemy hands.

Navigation practice was a priority and it came in plenty when the crews found themselves tasked with ferrying troops home from Italy. For most of these veterans this was their first flight and the Lancasters offered nothing in the way of comfort, just a seat on the floor and four blankets apiece. But it was also their first 'Blighty' leave for years and they were grateful. Twenty-seven passengers were dispersed around the aircraft in an arrangement carefully calculated about the Centre of Gravity and the order of taking up these positions was strictly laid down to maintain trim. The number was soon reduced to twenty, which eased the situation a little.

Another training exercise calling for intensive practice was high level bombing and day after day the Lancs circled and climbed before turning towards the Wainfleet range. Command ran into a snag with their plans to use H2S for this work. The High-gain Scanner designed for the job worked well enough but when the bomb doors opened the image was badly distorted.

One day, the Station Commander received a memo, surely from Flying Control, pointing out that Rose Cottage was inside the 15 degree limit of No.6 runway but carried no obstruction light. The groundwork of 1943 was repeated but in more detail, for it was discovered that the cottage stood on slightly rising ground and the top was actually 37.59 feet above the runway's end, breaking the 1 in 50 rule by over 100%. The letters passed to and fro and 5 Group Headquarters swiftly authorised the Superintendent Engineer to proceed. At the last moment, an on-site meeting was convened and the Station Commander, Site Engineer, and so on, assembled by the cottage. Someone with a good memory was also present and told how the original decision had been reached. The party gazed up at the trees then went off to lunch. Rose Cottage was spared the indigity of being topped by a red light and the Ministry saved forty-seven pounds, twelve shillings!

Another of the units assigned to Tiger Force was No.460 Squadron RAAF, and on July 27th they arrived at East Kirkby to join 57 in training. Despite the prospect of returning to the Pacific, the Australians left Binbrook with some regret after two years that held happy memories as well as sad. After their twenty Lancasters had flown out 'Binbrook looked, and felt, deserted.' They quickly settled into 5 and 6 Sites, recording that the new Station was 'a dispersed site, without the amenities of Binbrook, but is situated in very pleasant countryside.'

Though smaller than in the latter part of their Task Force days, Four-sixty was still established at 26 crews and half of these were sent on leave for the first week of August. Before the others could take their turn, Hiroshima was on everyone's lips. With the dropping of the atomic bombs the war, thankfully, came to a close.

With night flying now down to a minimum, some of the ground staff were able to put their backs into another job in the evenings. Picking up potatoes for the local farmers had certain attractions; two or three hours at half-a crown (12½p) per hour was well worth while and the free cider did not go down amiss.

On August 17th, Tiger Force training was halted and 460 joined 57 on their ferry work of Operation *Dodge*, flying to such places as Bari and Pomigliano.

The Avro Lincoln was to have been Bomber Command's prime weapon in Tiger Force and the first to enter squadron service, RF385, joined 57 Squadron on August 23rd, followed six days later by RF386 and RF387.

In appearance, the Lincoln owed much to her predecessor and was originally known as the Lancaster Mk.V, but was ten feet longer and had a wingspan eighteen feet greater. It carried half as much fuel again and was 50 mph faster at her cruising speed of 244 mph, though now the crews were learning to think in 'knots'. The crew make up was the same as for the Lancaster and on these earliest models only the armament of the mid-upper turret had changed, the ·303s giving way to ·5s.

Eight selected crews formed the Lincoln Conversion Flight, of which (now) Squadron Leaders Beetham and Jones and Flight Lieutenant Chatterton were founder members. Each pilot was to have ten hours training on the new type before commencing night flying. Evaluation trials were to be carried out in parallel with training and these trials demanded the maximum flying hours from each 'plane. Cross-country flights at varying heights up to 20,000 feet were in the planned programme but teething troubles, particularly with the Merlin 85 engines, soon put the target out of reach. From their arrival, none of the Lincolns were serviceable for a week and the three logged only nineteen hours between them during September. This was made up almost entirely of engine tests and 'circuits and bumps' for the crews, so that even the training programme was disrupted.

Meanwhile, the Lancasters continued their passenger flights, though some were stranded in Italy for weeks when heavy rains caused the metal mesh runways to become covered in mud. Even so, No.57 flew 560 troops home – and as many back – in September alone. The occupants of 57's PB884 had a lucky escape when she swung on take off from Bari and was written off, for no one was hurt.

Soon, 460 Squadron heard that they were to be disbanded and return home. On October 4th, their Commanding Officer, Wing Commander P.H. Swann DSO DFC, took off in AR: 'J-Jig' on the Squadron's last mission, to overfly the Australian War Memorial at Amiens. They were to take photographs and to pay homage to the Australians who died in the Great War, 1914-1918; secondly, in this last symbolic flight 'to pay tribute to the Lancaster bomber that has served us so well on many an operation.'

A parade and the inevitable party followed, but before leaving on October 10th the final report was submitted, thanking the RAF 'for hospitality, friendship and co-operation. ... now we lay down the weapons of war and prepare to rebuild the peace, strengthened by renewed ties with the Mother Country.'

Another notable departure from East Kirkby in October was the Station's longest serving Lancaster, LM517. DX:'C-Charlie' joined 57 in late March, 1944 and completed her war service with the raid on Berchtesgaden, her eightieth operation. In her early days she was not allocated to any particular crew but seemed to be the 'spare' Lanc. For example, she flew four operations in seventy hours in one period of July, '44, and took part in night or day ops for ten consecutive days in August. She served with the Royal Aircraft Establishment until December 1946, when she was broken up.

As the serviceability of the Lincolns improved a little RF386 made a trip of over two hours duration and '387 flew for nearly six hours on October 9th. Meanwhile, the crews were using '385 and had progressed onto four and three engine overshoots. The three Lincolns were airborne together, a unique occasion, for a photo call with one of the Lancasters in support of a Press release later in the month.

Engine problems continued to bug '386, but by the 23rd she seemed in better shape and was able to put in 4½ hours at 20,000 feet with '387. Four days later she and '385 were airborne for about seven hours, but this proved too much for her and the 'lame duck' was grounded for a month.

The other two Lincolns held the fort, but clocked up only forty hours between them in November, though this did include a notable occasion when they made a cross-country trip of 9 hours 20 minutes duration together.

Twice in five months 57 Squadron had seen the due regard paid to ceremony as other squadrons had been disbanded. In mid-November No.55 Base was closed. Seven three-man crews were posted from the Squadron to the staff of Station HQ, charged with the task of flying out the Lancasters, many of them bound for the scrapyard. As the aircraft left, 57's aircrew were simply 'posted out' and on 27th November No.57 Squadron was disbanded, a paper exercise only, for nothing was left.[1]

The Squadron could claim to have played its full part in the victory and to have paid its share of the price. In almost constant action since 1939, No.57 had carried out over 5,000 sorties for the loss of 172 of its various aircraft – Blenheims, Wellingtons and Lancasters. Nearly 200 awards for gallantry were made to the crews.

So the bombers left East Kirkby. The village had seen them go into battle and had shared the lives and sorrows of the men and women who had kept them in the air. One hundred and forty-eight of the Lancasters had been lost, along with over a thousand men, of whom, by the cold law of averages, more than half had died.

The Black Bullocks had departed.

[1] In contrast to this cursory dismissal, AOC No.1 Group (for 5 Group was on point of closure) took the salute at Scampton next day as, with all due ceremony, No.103 Squadron marched past and were stood down. Immediately, some of the crews reformed with those of the Lincoln Flight and returned to the Saluting Base as a brand new 57 Squadron.

Lincoln 'Y-Yoke', RF386, autumn 1945. Though matt black underneath, the white colour scheme was adopted for Tiger Force *(D. Brown)*

Swiftly the countless tons of equipment were dispersed. Load upon load of furniture from the NAAFI and elsewhere was taken to Barkston Heath and burnt. With no more aircraft fires to fight, Flight Lieutenant Grebby MBE found himself tasked with the disposal of 9,000 blankets and 3,000 bicycles! It was rumoured that there were farmers willing to pay two pounds for a good tarpaulin but did someone really get a tractor for fifty bob (£2.50)?

By Christmas, the staff was much reduced and all that could be spared were allowed home on leave. For those remaining, the traditions were kept up and they got their leave later.

'Demob' came early in the New Year for some of the 'older hands' and Jim Garraway went home to join Jean and the new baby (for his wife got an early release under the famous – or infamous, according to circumstances – 'Clause 11'). 'Mickey' got demobbed with another driver who was able to give him a home on a farm where he could have the freedom he had been used to.

The last 'plane, an Oxford that had been used as the Station hack, flew out on January 15th. By the end of the month the entire Station had been treated to a spring-clean. A unit of the Royal Army Service Corps were to take up residence in February and when their senior officers carried out an inspection all was in first class order. However, the wholesale takeover did not take place, though the army did make some use of the airfield for training drivers, and the Station went on to a 'Self-accounting Care and Maintenance' footing.

It was not long before Merlins were to be heard on the circuit once more. Coningsby was Base for two squadrons of Lancasters and one of Mosquitos and it was a convenient way of easing the congested airspace by making use of the empty runways nearby. Soon the Mosquitos of No.139 Squadron were regular visitors, using East Kirkby for their 'circuits and bumps'.

No.139 Squadron had gone to war early, for their Blenheims had taken off to photograph the German Fleet at noon on Sep-

Airspeed Oxford, AB722, of 231 OCU at East Kirkby, 1948. *(V. Hawley)*

Ground Staff aboard a David Brown tractor outside Workshops Headquarters, 231 OCU (as chalked on the wall), 1948. *(V. Hawley)*

tember 3rd, 'the day war broke out'. From 1943 they had flown 'Mossies' for 8 Group, the Pathfinder Force, and their training since the war had concentrated on this same role of low-level marking, plus low-angle bombing practice at Wainfleet.

By October 1946, the Coningsby runways were showing signs of wear and were declared unfit for aircraft weighing more than 25,000 lbs, which meant that the Lancasters and a few newly acquired Lincolns had to be moved elsewhere. A month later the runways began to break up, but this had no immediate effect on the Mosquitos, for by then they were all grounded for modification.

Once the dreadful blizzards Britain suffered in early 1947 were over total reliance was placed on East Kirkby while the necessary repairs were carried out at Coningsby. Most of 139's flying was carried out there, the aircraft only returning to Base for major and minor servicing. All the aircrew and most of the technical staff travelled in daily. Essential restoration work was put in hand, though with no great urgency, for the target date was set at mid-August.

On 14th March No.231 Operational Conversion Unit was formed at Coningsby, which was to double East Kirkby's useage. The new unit's purpose was to complement the role of 139, as the syllabus showed: 'Crews should be taught to find the target, mark the target, and return safely.' They were to be trained in procedures for stalling; flying, landing and mislanding on one engine (not yet known as 'asymmetric'); landing without flaps and dealing with fire in the air. There was also to be bombing and other special training.

Two crews were to be taken every three weeks, summer and winter. The initial training was to be given on Ansons (though Oxfords were also used), seven hours day flying and fourteen at night. There followed a similar period of day flying on the Mosquitos and eighteen at night.

All this was the concern of the Chief Flying Instructor. The Chief Ground Instructor's brief was a reminder that this was a peacetime Service: 'Students will be required to take pride in their Service, their uniform and their brevet. Any slackness observed must be remedied'.

The crew members, pilots and navigators, appeared to lose all rank whilst under training and were identified by their work and course number, thus : P2 Smith, N3 Jones, etc.

'The move to East Kirkby is well under way', reported the Signals Section in July. 'By August full facilities will be available: full flarepath lighting on all runways, power and 'phone to the Air Traffic Control caravan and adequate telephones installed on the Technical Site.'

So it was. No.2 Course started their flying from East Kirkby in August and an inspection at the time reported that the radio and radar facilities were 'very good'. By now a Servicing Flight had moved in and the entire Coningsby flying commitment was being carried out at the detached airfield.

All ran smoothly for months, apart from a crash by one of the OCU Mosquitos after a heavy landing. There were no casualties, apart from the aircraft, which had to be sent back to de Havillands.

Christmas was a more leisurely affair now and the Station closed for a week. Not everyone went home, however, for it was recorded, probably by one of the 'losers', that 'Flight 'Lieutenant Lingard won (?) the draw for Station Duty Officer'.

On 3rd February 1948, the Works Engineer told a familiar story: the runways had begun to crumble, and the airfield was closed next day. The repairs at Coningsby were sufficiently advanced and the aircraft returned to their home Base.

Within a fortnight East Kirkby was reduced to an unmanned satellite. In these days of terrorists, vandals and other cranks it may be surprising to learn that there were still large stocks of bombs, quite unattended, in the Station bomb store. In 1945 Coningsby had been made responsible for these and for the even larger quantity at Spilsby. Periodic examiniation by Armament Inspection Teams ensured that the stores were not deteriorating but the preparation and removal was a strain on resources. The country was flooded with Government surplus equipment at the time, yet incredibly there was no crane available for some weeks and a great deal of manhandling had to be done at Spilsby, where there were nearly a hundred 4,000 pounders.

In July, 1948, a start was made on the East Kirkby holdings which included nearly five hundred 500-lb 'General Purpose' bombs and in a couple of months all the weapons and components had been cleared.

East Kirkby airfield went to sleep.

Mosquitos of 231 OCU at East Kirkby, *above* with Mosquito B. XVI PF602 in the background and *below,* ML983, coded 'O-Oboe'. *(both V. Hawley)*

Chapter Ten

The 1950s – and the USAF

By 1950 the old station was a sorry sight. The accommodation huts had been sold off – £20 would have bought a 'Nissen', £30 a 'Seco', less bases of course. 'Care and Maintenance' had proved empty words and other buildings had fallen into disrepair. Weeds grew in the cracks, and expansion joints of the concrete, the runways were marked with large crosses denoting 'Closed to aircraft' and as if in sympathy, Old Bolingbroke mill shed a sail.

It was a year since the Russians had recognised the futility of the Berlin blockade but world peace remained in a fragile state (the Korean conflict began in June 1950) and the United States began to extend its nuclear capabilities so as to reach 'any target that might need such treatment' as it was chillingly phrased. To do this, they planned to have a fleet of bombers at instant readiness, some airborne, others standing by, for every hour of every day, all under the control of their Strategic Air Command. Accordingly, to augment the home bases in the States, a worldwide chain of airfields was being prepared, from the Arctic to the Far East. The 'European' theatre included Spain, North Africa, Turkey and, of course, America's staunchest ally, Britain.

In early 1951 the British Government agreed to a special construction programme to provide the USAF with additional airfields in the UK. This work, largely funded by the Americans would give the USAF bases for use by Strategic Air Command. The organisation of the USAF in the UK was changed to reflect the build up and its title of 3rd Air Division was upgraded to 3rd Air Force. A new 7th Air Division was formed to support the visiting bomber units.

The restoration of suitable airfields was soon put in hand and East Kirkby was among the first of such properties to be put at the disposal of the USAF. The major work to be undertaken on most of the airfields was the lengthening of at least one runway, for the Boeing B-47 Stratojet bomber about to come into service had a ponderously long take off run. At East Kirkby the 08/26 runway was extended to the ENE by 3,800 feet, almost doubling its length and taking it way past the old bomb store to within a few hundred yards of the A16 Boston-Spilsby road. This called for a further mile and a quarter of perimeter track and the old gardener's cottage was the first casualty. The wartime practice of aircraft dispersal was abandoned and a giant 'Mass Aircraft Park', measuring some 350 yards square was laid on a hardcore foundation fifteen feet thick, lying across the original main runway close by the former 55 Base hangars.

As refurbishment of the technical buildings was put in hand, new living quarters and a Base Hospital were built where the former Base and Station HQ had been. A noticeable improvement in the standard of the living accomodation was the provision of central heating. It was not that the earlier occupants of bomber fields were of a hardier breed, merely that the USAF took the view that the constant colds and respiratory problems that had plagued such places were not conducive to efficiency.

By April 1954 the contractors' work was virtually finished and on the 17th the 3931st Air Base Group of 7th Air Division moved in. Their preparatory work was complete by July and 3917th ABG took over to act as parent unit for the operational squadrons, though the first of these did not arrive until early 1955.

Despite the huge runway, East Kirkby was not destined to play host to the bombers but was designated a Reserve Airfield and accommodated units of the Military Air Transport Service offering search, rescue and evacuation support to the force.

It was the practice in Strategic Air Command at the time to rotate operational units between bases, completing a ninety day tour on each. Subsequently, the 61st, 63rd and 64th Air Rescue Squadrons followed this routine, each leaving East Kirkby at the end of its three month stint to be replaced by one of the others.

The squadrons flew Douglas SC-47s, readily recognisable to British eyes as the ubiquitous Dakota and which, among its many roles had served as a flying ambulance in all theatres during the late war. The ample fuselages of the SAC aircraft were fitted to carry up to thirty stretchers. They were also fitted with extra fuel tanks for the long-range work required of them and had an AUW (all up weight) of a surprising 73,000 lbs – well in excess of the operational Lancasters that preceded them. Thus, they made good use of the extended runway, but if called upon to effect an evacuation from an inhospitable situation it was unlikely that a mile and a half of level ground would be available. The problem was taken care of by fitting three rocket motors to the tail. These gave such impetus to the aircraft that she lifted off at an angle of about forty degrees and a practice emergency take off was a most impressive spectacle.

The impact on the village when the new incumbents arrived was hardly less than when the RAF had moved in eleven years earlier. Certainly, the road traffic increased. The RAF had acquired Revesby Abbey, a mile or so along the road, as officers' quarters and the USAF took over these apartments. Additionally, some of the Base personnel lived with their families in Skegness hotels and drove to work daily. On frosty mornings the East Keal schoolboys would watch the commuters drive their oversized Pontiacs and 'Chevvies' down

The extended main runway *(F. T. Bailey)*

the sweeping bend towards the airfield, fiendishly waiting for the unwary to discover the ice. Sometimes their patience was rewarded with two or three spectacular spins before the victim ran off the road.

The aim was then, as now, that each Base should be self-sufficient and in time a school was erected on the Technical Site for the newcomers' children. Again, in line with contemporary practice, all ranks were encouraged to foster good relations locally and join in with village events where possible, though with the various Clubs (Messes) and the shopping facilities at the PX it was easy enough for an airman to live quite happily in this little America, without going 'off-Base'.

Not surprisingly, the lure of the bright lights proved too much. Most of the enlisted men had been drafted for National Service, often straight from school. These brash young men were seeing the world for the first time, determined to enjoy the experience and they soon discovered the power of the mighty dollar. The RAF's 'erks' of a decade earlier had to get by on five or six shillings (25p-30p) per day and, Stateside, the GIs would have been little better off. Over here, with the considerable duty-free concessions on Base and relaxation of purchase tax in British shops, they found that $100 a month and an exchange rate of about $2.70 to the pound made them rich. Many a local farmworker had no more to raise his family on.

Overcoming the alleged dislike of 'warm' beer, the airmen all but monopolised the

Red Lion and other pubs in the locality. For those of a serious bent, such places as the 'original' Boston were bound to be an attraction and, touring the immediate district some must have come across the handful of cottages that glory under the name of 'New York', a very little 'Apple'. The newcomers had the advantage over the station's previous residents, in that the signposts removed under threat of invasion had been restored. (Perhaps one of our American cousins was author of the inspired graffiti added to the signpost by the A155: 'To Old Bolingbroke & Mavis Enderby' '- a son'?) East Kirkby did not quite become another Klondyke with the arrival of the free-spending 'Yanks' but there was money to be made and a Hamburger Bar was soon built near the Main Gate. One local entrepreneur invested in a second hand Ford Consul as a taxi and 'clocked' 100,000 miles in the first twelve months for Lincoln was a popular night spot and a cab each way the natural thing to do. Walter Handson, retired from the licenced trade, had established his butcher's shop across the road. The cutting-up of the weekly ration of 1/2d (6p) worth of fresh meat for each of his customers was a thing of the past. Now he had new customers, like the Master Sergeant known locally as 'Smokey Joe', whose regular demand was for 'a pound and a half of chuck steak to round off the helluva of a good weekend I got planned'.

The self-sufficiency of the Base was incomplete in one aspect, for feminine company was in short supply. When a dance was to be held, the remedy was to make up the shortfall by despatching a coach to Nottingham, 'the city of pretty girls', and bus in a few dozen partners – an impossible scheme for wartime days, for had the coach and its fuel been available the Nottingham lasses already had their pick of the thousands of soldiers and airmen stationed in the area.

Many of the local girls were quite enchanted by these boys, their parents sometimes less so. Despite opposition romance blossomed, successful marriages took place and, in due course, half a dozen or more of a new generation of GI brides crossed the Atlantic.

The village saw a little of the seamier side of life for inevitably camp followers put in an appearance, but generally the 'goings on' at the 'drome were a cause for amusement rather than any other reaction. The Base's commitment to rescue operations that, with luck, would never be called upon, engendered boredom.

With twenty years of sterling service behind it there can have been few multi-engined aircraft less demanding in man hours for routine servicing than the Dakota. While the ground staff waited, the aircrews carried out their long patrols, though they did not enjoy the comparative comfort of pressurised cabins such as were occupied by those aboard the bombers and tankers whose welfare they looked to. While the bombers circled the Polar wastes and the North Atlantic, the crews of the SC-47s pursued their vigil forty-odd thousand feet below, beneath the threshold of Soviet radar. They flew predetermined routes in complete radio silence and as it was essential that the precise position of each aircraft was known to Command at all times navigation was handled by an augmented team.

By 1956 the workload was falling; many units of 7th AD re-equipped with fighter-bombers and the strength of the Division was almost halved.

Since the war's end, East and West had been engaged in a race to produce the ultimate weapon, the ICBM (Inter-Continental Ballistic Missile) to carry a nuclear warhead. By 1957 the race was run – there could never be a winner, only losers – and the silos began to sprout around the world. A year later, concrete was being poured to house the Thor missiles that were to rear their nosecones over airfields that had last seen war as their Lancasters went into battle.

By 1958 the earlier phase of Strategic Air Command's task was being run down and the USAF began to withdraw from East Kirkby. On 1st August 'Old Glory' and the RAF Ensign beside it were lowered for the last time. The Americans took away everything that could be moved and the airfield was handed back to be abandoned once more before the year was out.

Chapter Eleven

Back to the Plough

It has been seen how, under the pressures of war, the Air Ministry was far from tardy in taking whatever land it wanted. It is still evident in the 'eighties how reluctant Whitehall can be in parting with its land. Some pre-war RAF stations have been handed over to the Army and others turned into prisons - a few disconsolate conscripts might claim that they always were! Some of the wartime fields are still in Government hands, presumably in case they might 'come in handy', though it can hardly have been envisaged that the hangars would provide cover for some of the European grain mountain.

When the USAF folded its tents and left, East Kirkby had served its purpose but for years the Air Ministry was content to play the part of the country landlord, lettting out such of the land as they saw fit, for agriculture. In September, 1964, they offered 199 acres for sale. Due to constraints placed by existing leases, growing crops, etc, the land to be sold comprised odd pieces scattered around the site. Four of the lots, ranging in size from 23 to 53 acres and situated at the end of the runway extension in one case to 630 Squadron's old dispersal points at the other extreme, were all described as Arable Holdings of 'freeworking medium loam which will grow heavy crops of Potatoes, Sugar Beet and all kinds of Cereals.'

One lot, of 27 acres, was described as a Freehold Site and consisted of about two-thirds of the old Technical Site, including the Control Tower and the base of No.57 Squadron's No.2 Hangar, dismantled previously. Gone also were two of the four 'Base Hangars', No.4, furthest from the road, and No.7, the odd one out, in that it

had been a MAP B2-type. The remaining two were offered in separate lots, described as 'T2 Hangar and site'. No.6 was already let to a transport company but the rest of the property was sold with vacant possession, the existing leases being due to expire at Michaelmas, the traditional end to the farming year. Twelve months later a second sale was held and this time the rest of the airfield, about 650 acres, came onto the market. As before, the venue, the White Hart Hotel, Spilsby, was packed to capacity, for the auctions aroused a great deal of interest among the local farming community, particularly among those with hopes of recovering land they had farmed before. Generally they were to be disappointed for bidding was keen and the prices realised were beyond the pockets of most. Despite the large areas of concrete, the land fetched over £150 per acre, a hefty sum for those days.

When the contractors arrived in 1942 they swept away all before them, but for centuries the parochial bounds between East Kirkby and Hagnaby had been marked by a footpath. This ran from the road junction southwards for over a mile and a half, curiously within only yards of the Greenwich Meridian. For the purpose of the sales the obvious divisions of the land formed by runways and so on were disregarded and, as far as possible, the lots were marked out and identified by the old 'Enclosure' numbers of the Ordnance Survey. All trace of the footpath had gone but its line formed the western boundary of the largest plot, some 220 acres, probably equivalent to twenty-five or thirty of the original fields. One boundary of another plot was so fixed as to include a yard wide strip from the edge of a runway.

The entire 'Base Hangar' area eventually came into the hands of a potato packing company and in the 'seventies they brought in similar hangars from Yorkshire so that four were to be seen once more in their new role as warehouses. Another company erected chicken-rearing units on the old Admin and Technical Sites, as well as on a small plot across the airfield, but in general cultivation continued as before.

Over the years various new owners have adopted differing policies towards the runways and perimeter track. During 1974, as the last of the T2 hangars was being erected on the former Base Maintenance area, contractors were brought in to tear up some of the runways. There was a big demand for construction materials at this time and farmers were finding that crushed concrete from former airfields was a lucrative 'crop'. The contractors removed many of the former dispersals and reduced the width of the former subsidiary runway 12/30 to a single-track road. The 08/26 runway, that which was extended in the 'fifties, was also reduced in width to a farm road with the exception of the extension itself. The owners of the extension have done nothing to remove the concrete and it, with its perimeter tracks, remains today. Whilst the tracks have become cluttered with rubble brought to the surface by ploughing, the runway remains in excellent condition. Strangely, the 2,000 yard wartime main runway (02/20) was left intact, perhaps because of the huge aircraft parking area built across its northern end. It was not until 1986 that contractors began to remove part of this runway but little was done before work ceased.

With so much clear space and the availability of good runways, East Kirkby has become a popular site for general and sporting aviation . Two centres of activity have evolved on the airfield, one using the runway, the other using the mass parking area, or 'square', as it is known locally, for take off and landing.

The long and smooth runway has proved popular as a forward operating base for aerial spraying aircraft belonging to a number of companies. Throughout the spring and early summer crop spraying 'planes are often to be seen using the runway, sometimes as many as three different companies working side by side. Piper Pawnees are most regularly seen at East Kirkby, though the long runway has proved attractive to operators of the big Schweizer Ag-Cats.

Recreational flying is a growing activity and since 1980 the East Kirkby Soaring Group has flown various types of gliders off the field. Over the years these have included interesting craft such as a Grunau Baby and an EoN 460. By early 1987 a hangar had been erected near the runway to house two ex-Air Training Corps Slingsby T-21 gliders bought from the RAF.

East Kirkby's main runway being slowly reduced to rubble. *(W. J. Taylor)*

'Maximum Effort', July 1978. Pawnees prepare for operations *(W. J. Taylor)*

'Bombing-up', April 1978. Loading a Pawnee with granular fertiliser *(W. J. Taylor)*

The wide open spaces around the runway have attracted both hang glider and microlight aircraft enthusiasts. The hang gliders are towed aloft by a vehicle driving along the perimeter track whilst the microlights take to the air from the runway. At weekends, both of these relatively new forms of sport aviation are in full swing, operating alongside and in close harmony with the gliders. Indeed, such is the friendly atmosphere of co-operation between the users of the airfield that crop sprayers can be seen working at the same time as the part time pilots.

Because of the relatively cluttered surroundings and poor approaches, aerial activity from the square has been much different. The aircraft operating from here have generally been privately owned and flown, such as Cessna 150s and 172s, though Pawnees and Ag-Cats have landed to park overnight by the Tower. The description 'deserted airfield' hardly rings true.

After leaving East Kirkby, No.57 Squadron soldiered on, with only short breaks in service. After years as part of the nuclear V-Bomber Force, the Squadron moved to Marham in 1965 with its Handley Page Victors, to convert to a new role as air-to-air tankers. Ten years later in March 1975 the Squadron suffered a tragedy, when during a night refuelling exercise over the North Sea, a Buccaneer collided with the tail of one of its Victor tankers. Amazingly, the smaller aircraft was able to return to its base virtually unscathed but the entire tail unit was torn off the Victor and she plunged into the sea ninety miles off Newcastle. The captain, Flight Lieutenant K.I. Handscomb, managed to eject and was picked up, injured, from the sea, but his four companions were lost. This sad accident formed a common bond between past and serving members of the Squadron when they met a few weeks later. The late Len Tolfts, a former air-gunner with 630 Squadron, placed a 'small ad' in the RAF Association journal *Air Mail* proposing that a reunion and memorial service be held in the village. The idea met with a gratifying response and, on Sunday 4th May, fifty or so former members of the two Squadrons gathered in the village hall.

Many brought their wives and the occasion was made complete when they were joined by a coachload of serving airmen and their families from Marham, led by their Commanding Officer, Wing Commander A. Sutherland.

The little church was packed as the 57 Squadron Standard was laid up on the altar for the service conducted by the Reverend Bob Cave, a former corporal electrician on the station. A host of local folk gathered too, when wreaths were laid at the foot of the old Control Tower, which was serving as an office for the contractors whose machines were to be seen, even at that moment, across the field, devouring vast tracts of concrete in a cloud of dust.

The tower itself was a windowless shell, its days surely numbered, and to many who witnessed the simple ceremony it must have appeared that an end had come to the links between the village and the RAF. But old friendships were renewed that day and new ones made; such ties as had remained between the village and those who had served there were strengthened enormously and many of those involved kept in touch.

In 1979, Jerry Monk, one half of 630's 'Holy War', took over the reins and on the foundations laid by Len Tolfts, the 57 and 630 Squadrons (1939-46) Association was formed. Plans were made to raise a memorial to those who died while flying from the airfield and with contributions from home and abroad, the small sum of money accrued at the time of the earlier event was soon multipled ten-fold. A great deal of help, both practical and financial, came from friends in the East Kirkby area, not least the offer of a suitable site by Messrs Panton Bros, the company that had acquired the chicken-rearing business.

On Sunday, 7th October 1979, over five hundred people assembled to see Wing Commander Roger Betts, Officer Commanding No.57 Squadron, unveil the memorial on the site of the guardroom that had stood by the entrance to the airfield – a fitting tribute to those who had flown from this quiet corner of Lincolnshire, never to return.

IN MEMORY OF
THOSE WHO GAVE
THEIR LIVES WITH
57 AND 630
SQUADRONS
1939 – 1945

LEAKE

The memorial, with detail of the text of the left and right hand tablets.
(all photographs J. Monk)

OLD AIRFIELD

I LIE HERE, STILL, BESIDE THE HILL,
ABANDONED LONG TO NATURE'S WILL,
MY BUILDINGS DOWN, MY PEOPLE GONE,
MY ONLY SOUNDS, THE WILD BIRDS SONG.

BUT MY MIGHTY BIRDS WILL RISE NO MORE,
NO MORE I HEAR THE MERLINS ROAR,
AND NEVER NOW MY BOSOM FEELS,
THE POUNDING OF THEIR GIANT WHEELS.

FROM THE AGELESS HILL THEIR VOICES CAST,
THUNDEROUS ECHOES OF THE PAST,
AND STILL, IN LONELY REVERIE,
THEIR GREAT DARK WINGS SWEEP DOWN TO ME.

LAUGHTER, SORROW, HOPE, AND PAIN,
I SHALL NEVER KNOW THESE THINGS AGAIN,
EMOTIONS THAT I CAME TO KNOW,
OF STRANGE YOUNG MEN SO LONG AGO.

WHO KNOWS, AS EVENING SHADOWS MEET,
ARE THEY WITH ME STILL, A PHANTOM FLEET,
AND DO MY GHOSTS STILL STRIDE, UNSEEN,
ACROSS MY FACE, SO WIDE AND GREEN.

AND IN THE FUTURE, SHOULD STRUCTURES TALL,
BURY ME BEYOND RECALL,
I SHALL STILL REMEMBER THEM,
MY METAL BIRDS, AND LONG-DEAD MEN.

NOW WEEDS GROW HIGH, OBSCURE THE SKY,
O REMEMBER ME, WHEN YOU PASS BY,
FOR BENEATH THIS TANGLED, LEAFY SCREEN,
I WAS YOUR HOME, YOUR FRIEND, "SILKSHEEN"

W. SCOTT.
EX–630 SQUADRON.

MEMBERS OF NOS. 57 AND 630 SQUADRONS
WHO ERECTED THIS MEMORIAL PAY TRIBUTE
TO THE PEOPLE OF EAST KIRKBY WHO
MADE THEM WELCOME IN BOTH WAR
AND THE PEACE THAT FOLLOWED AND
GENEROUSLY CONTRIBUTED TO THE
MEMORIAL FUND.
THIS MEMORIAL STANDS ON THE
SITE OF THE GUARD ROOM OF THE
AIRFIELD FROM WHICH BOTH SQUADRONS
OPERATED BETWEEN AUGUST 30TH 1943 AND
APRIL 25TH 1945 AND FROM WHICH
OVER 1000 AIR CREW 'WENT MISSING'.

OCTOBER 1979.

Chapter Twelve

Silksheen's Future
A Tribute to the Past

For years the thirty miles of branch line which ran from Lincoln to its junction with the Boston-Louth railway was the very lifeline of the district. By 1944, a list of some of the little towns and villages it served read like a Bomber Command Battle Order: Fiskerton, Bardney, Woodhall Spa, Coningsby, East Kirkby. For the last, Stickney Halt was the 'railhead' and, of the thousands posted there the vast majority would have arrived on the little train that puffed its way steadily across the Fens. In the station yard they piled their kit-bags – how many containing flying kit were returned by lorry, to be thrown into a goods van? – and looked around for transport. Anything would do, motor-bike, jeep, crew bus or staff car, as long as it bore Five Group's 'B/5' on the front mudguard.

The rural lines were swept away years ago but little else has changed, least of all the flat landscape with 'Boston Stump', the famous tower of St Botolph's, standing as proud as ever, nine miles to the south. If one approaches East Kirkby from this direction nowadays the hangar/warehouses come into view long before traces of the airfield itself are seen. As with other airfield sites, the most notable evidence of past useage is the absence of fences, hedges or drains (dykes), leaving huge fields well suited to modern farming. To the left lies a simple part of everyday life, a sewage works. In October 1944, Flying Control had another of their grumbling sessions: 'On an airfield accomodating forty-three Lancasters and three Hurricanes' (for fighter affiliation practice) 'the sewage works at the WSW end of two runways constitutes a serious obstacle, but it is appreciated that its removal at

this stage of the war is a practical impossibility.' The site of the filter beds and other plant was not well chosen but they survived the countless tons of high explosives that had passed a hundred feet above them and have performed their mundane task for the benefit of the local community ever since, one of the better legacies.

Drawing closer to the village, new bungalows appear along Fen Road, some of them on the land where Helmut earned his new shoes. Kirkby Cross is as neat and tidy as ever around the War Memorial that records the village's more personal sacrifices in past wars. Just across the road, Mrs Edna Ely, née Vickers, still lives at Woodbine Cottage where she treasures the Squadrons' visitors' book and is delighted to welcome the many who return to the village that holds so many memories. Down towards the church some of No.1 Site remains. The Gymnasium is now a frozen food store and a few lesser buildings survive but the rest is a clutter of bricks and concrete beneath the trees. In contrast, close by is No.1 Building, a neat bungalow, just as it was when it began life as the Station Commander's Residence, and looking very well for 'Temporary Brick'.

Inaccessible as they are, the bases of the huts on the living sites have not been removed and the layout can still be traced. A shoe toe scuffled through the leaves and debris of forty years reveals glazed tiles in the gulley of an 'ablutions block' as white as the day they were laid, whilst here and there, rusted from their bases, are a few of the ornate iron boot-scrapers that stood by every door.

Returning to the main road, one passes 'Two Comm' and the old Admin Site, still occupied by chicken houses. At the junction stands a service station and further along is another, converted from the Hamburger Grill. Will they ever serve as much petrol as flowed through the pumps that stood nearby? Hour after hour the long grey 'Pool' tankers arrived, each with 2,000 gallons of 100 octane fuel and each 154 gallons short of a full load for a greedy Lancaster.

East Kirkby - the old gym and chapel on Command Site 1. *(F. T. Bailey)*

The Station Commanders residence - still habitable - the tower on the left is East Kirkby Mill. *(W. J. Taylor)*

The Control Tower is in the centre of this fine aerial view taken in May 1979. It is flanked by the bases of the 'squadron' hangars though the base of No.1 has since been removed. The white buildings by the perimeter track are chicken units. To the extreme right can be seen part of 'The Square'. *(W. J. Taylor)*

The warehouses dominate this end of the village though the potato handling business, now a part of the giant Ross Group, occupies only about ten acres of the site. The juggernauts that roll onto the weighbridge bring in some 60,000 tons of potatoes a year, the produce of the eastern side of England that was once known as 'Bomber Country'. With the further buildings since added and the refrigeration facilities available the year-round operation pre-packs and distributes the homely 'spuds' to many of the Nation's supermarkets. No one would deny that the buildings are an eyesore and will remain so, at least until the young trees that have been planted mature, but farming these days has moved beyond the scene of a few old hens scratching around a hayrick. East Kirkby needs to make a living and while the nation retains its appetite for chicken and chips the future looks assured.

By the crossroads the Red Lion still proclaims and serves 'Bateman's Good Honest Ales', though not from a bucket. The outside is little changed but within, things have moved with the times. A pool table occupies what was once the butcher's shop and the 'public' is larger now that a passage wall has been removed, making room for a 'one-armed bandit' – happily, the only 'Bandit' on the East Kirkby circuit nowadays. Back in place after years of banishment is the ancient round table, its medieval simplicity marred by the scratchings of 1944. Syd Smith has gone down to posterity.

Every couple of years or so the village gladly suffers an invasion when the 'old uns' come back in force. In the pub the halves of bitter are sipped slowly, for there is much to be said. While log-books and albums are studied, the ageing features of their owners are being compared with long treasured photos of younger men, produced from handbags along with shiny colour snaps of grandchildren.

'I don't know if they know it,' said one local worthy, 'but to us in Lincolnshire, the aircrew lads will always be something special; very special people.' His words are borne out by the throng of folk from the district who join them at the memorial later. Around the lowered Standards they stand, in a silence broken only by the passing cars, homeward bound from Skegness. Among the wreathes, red, white and blue, lies a bunch of wild flowers picked from the airfield by a lady, still trim in the green and khaki of the Womens' Land Army, 'for the boys'. They Grow Not Old... .

If any old eyes remain dry they may water a little from gazing up at the sky as the Lancaster 'City of Lincoln' approaches. She turns around the old mill as so many have before and sweeps low over the Control Tower, the roar of her Merlins sweet music to ears that complain of noisy pop groups. She circles again and dips her wings; no one moves until that unforgetable silhouette is but a speck over Coningsby.

For other times and other visitors, the memorial serves as a reminder for the curious and a datum point for those returning 'for old times sake.' Nicely maintained, with a backcloth of Leylandii growing taller year by year, it is a source of pride to the people of East Kirkby and beyond, particulary to those who witnessed the stirring events and shared the shattering grief of the earliest days of the Royal Air Force Station it commemorates.

All traces of the guardroom have vanished but the MT workshops still stand and beyond are a couple of bungalows. Two light aircraft often make their home nearby on neatly trimmed grass but to the right, nature had taken back her own by 1984. Young trees and undergrowth spread around the concrete bases where the squadron hangars, Nos.1 & 2, had stood, screening the Control Tower from view.

Twice the tower has been allowed to fall into disrepair but, with a determination to save what he can of the little that is left of Bomber Command, farmer Fred Panton decided to set about its preservation. External restoration was soon completed and internal refurbishment continues.

Something of the airfield's history gained national attention when a programme written by Jack Currie DFC, author and former Lancaster pilot, was shown on BBC TV. During 1985 he interviewed a

Above, the control tower in November 1970. The lettering on the first floor wall dates from the USAF days as does the fire/crash tender house beyond. *Below,* following its restoration a miniature signals square has been built in front of the Watch Office. The original signals square was partially covered by a concrete roadway to the crash tender shed during American occupation *(both W.J. Taylor)*

number of local people whose stories concerned curious phenomena each had experienced at various times – strange figures seen walking easily across ploughed land where paths had once been, the sound of returning Lancasters in early morning and of unexplained footsteps climbing the stairs of the Watch Tower, which lent its name to that interesting and evocative production. The supernatural is something on which each must make up his own mind though even sceptics have admitted to feeling a strange chill or presence at scenes of long-past battles such as Glencoe.

There was nothing intangible about the Lancaster that was in Fred and Harold Panton's sights as they entered negotiations to purchase the one known as 'The Scampton Lanc'. The varied history of this Lancaster has been well recorded. Built in 1945, NX611 was intended for 'Tiger Force' but lay in store until 1951. Following conversion to suit her for maritime patrol work she joined the *Aéronavale*, the French Naval Air Service. She served for ten years, first in Brittany then Morocco and after a major overhaul, flew out to the Pacific to continue her work from New Caledonia.

Two years later the French Government decided to retire the last of their Lancasters and the British based Historic Aircraft Preservation Society tried to acquire one. They were given 'WU-15', as she then was,

free of all charge, but were faced with a daunting fund-raising task to finance the cost of bringing her home from Australia. Their efforts were successful and after a flight of 13,000 miles, NX611 (civil registered as G-ASXX) arrived at Biggin Hill in May 1965.

For the next two years extensive – not to say expensive – work was carried out, but she flew on few occasions. Much credit is due to the HAPS but the financial strain proved too much and the Society folded. Under new owners, she eventually arrived at Hullavington, where more work was carried out before an Airworthiness Certificate for 'One Flight Only' was granted. It was planned for her to be the star of an exhibition at Blackpool and she landed at Squire's Gate on 26th June 1970. This proved to be her last flight and she soon became a white elephant once more, lying exposed to the weather and the salt-laden air for two years.

Rescue came when the Right Honourable Lord Lilford of Nateby purchased the aircraft. Fred Panton had been a prospective buyer and, being keen to see a Lancaster displayed in his home county, persuaded the Royal Air Force to take an interest. Lord Lilford lent her to them on long term loan and she was dismantled and taken to Scampton in August, 1975. Eight months and hundreds of voluntary man-hours later she was put in place to grace the entrance of this famous station.

Opposite: 'Lucky Charlie' DX:C, LM517, outside No.2 Hangar. The photo was taken from the Electrical/Instrument Section in the summer of 1945, when the convention of painting the 'tail number' under the wing was adopted. *(L. G. Wakerell)*

Above: No.2 Hangar now reduced to a base only, taken from the balcony of the Control Tower in 1987. *(F. T. Bailey)*

Below: NX611 at Blackpool on 26th June 1970. Her Historic Aircraft Preservation Society code HA-P has been replaced by GL-C to honour Geoffrey Leonard Cheshire VC. On her move to Scampton she was marked YF-C, the code given to Guy Gibson's aircraft whilst on the 'Station Flight'. All codes are in Oxide Red to approximate the original red dope. *(Brian Goulding via author)*

The new hangar, although of modern construction, is built on the original foundations of a T2 site. Behind the propeller and replica ROC post are two wooden barrack huts recently acquired from Manby *(both W. J. Taylor)*

Soon there came news that the hopes of the Panton brothers might be fulfilled and they would be able to achieve their ambition to provide NX611 with a permanent home under cover, so to evoke nostalgia in older folk and, perhaps, to bring wonder to generations yet to come.

As these developments were taking shape, 1986 brought unhappy news from other quarters. Though formed in 1916, No.57 Squadron was still the 'junior' of the tanker units, and with their Victors set for a premature de-mob (due mainly to the exceptionally high utilisation rates necessary during the Falklands conflict) and their anticipated replacement in the service by fewer, newer, larger aircraft, the word came to disband. When the decision was first made known, the Queen, on a visit to Marham, expressed the hope that

the Phoenix may yet rise again. All who witnessed the impressive, but sad, last parade on 30th June would echo Her Majesty's sentiments, none more so than the many old 'Bomber Boys' present.

The Lincolnshire Aviation Museum had been settled at Tattershall, just seven miles from East Kirkby, for some years. The origins of the museum dated back to about 1967, when the engines of a Heinkel He 111 were recovered from the beach at Chapel St Leonards, near Skegness, where they had lain buried since 1940. These formed the beginning of a considerable collection built up over the years by a number of enthusiasts and accommodation was always a problem.

To their assistance came Fred and Harold Panton of Stickford, with the offer of a building in which to house more of their exhibits and in 1980 John Chatterton DFC, who still farms locally, opened the *Panton Wing*, named in memory of Sergeant Christopher Panton (who, as the eldest of four brothers, was the Flight Engineer of a No.433 Squadron Halifax which failed to return from the infamous Nuremburg raid, the day after his appointment to Pilot Officer was confirmed).

There was further extension to the Museum in 1982 when an authentic Nissen hut was erected, along with other imaginative exhibits, such as a replica of a Royal Observer Corps observation post.

In 1987 there came a painful blow to those who had expended so much energy in this admirable enterprise when they found that they were unable to renew the lease on the premises where they were established. Once more the Panton generosity took a practical form with the offer of accommodation for much of their Museum's collection. The Nissen hut was soon re-sited and work to transfer the display material was swiftly under way.

Meanwhile, the Panton brothers were making progress with their own plans. The erection of three wooden barrack huts from the old RAF Station at Manby provided more working and display space but the most visible progress was made early in 1988 when a new hangar was put up on

The main entrance to the Aviation Heritage Centre is dominated by the new hangar.
(W. J. Taylor)

The magnitude of the task of moving an aircraft the size of the Lancaster and the amount of equipment to achieve the task without damage can be clearly seen.
(W. J. Taylor)

Group Captain Leonard Cheshire unveils a portrait of Roy Chadwick, designer of the Lancaster, at East Kirkby in front of NX611, on 30th April 1991. *(P. H. T. Green)*

the site of 57 Squadron's old Number One 'T2'. Although of modern construction and, at present, only half the length of the original, the building took East Kirkby one more step along the way back to its 1943 appearance.

But the enterprise took a giant stride at the end of April, 1988, when the major sections of NX611 arrived, conveyed on no less than seven 'Queen Mary' transports. Three lesser loads followed and by mid-May a complete Lancaster had returned to the old bomber field. Over the following weeks a team from RAF Abingdon set about re-assembling the aircraft.

Keen to encourage tourism, the County Council has inaugurated the sign-posting of an 'Aviation Tourist Trail' to guide

visitors with such interests around the county. As well as the old airfield sites and the various memorials that have been raised, they will inevitably see something of the operational bases and at Coningsby, in particular, there is much to see, for a joint RAF/County Council venture already presents the famous *Battle of Britain Memorial Flight* to the public.

Already a great attraction on the route, The Lincolnshire Aviation Heritage Centre, East Kirkby, was formally opened in July 1989, by Marshal of the Royal Air Force Sir Michael Beetham GCB, CBE, DFC, AFC. Protected from the elements for the first time in over forty-five years, NX611 forms the centrepiece of the attractions, in the company of a number of contemporary vehicles, an intriguing display of artefacts and an ever-increasing collection of photographs.

Though but a small portion of the original airfield, there is plenty of space for the visitor to roam at will. All round the site are little reminders of those past days, while in the Control Tower the restoration of the Watch Office has captured the atmosphere of an 'ops' night.

Another notable collection on display is the unique assembly of memorabilia and archives belonging to the Royal Air Force Escaping Society. Well presented in its own building, it tells a little of the stories of airmen who escaped from captivity and of the incredible bravery of the men and women of the resistance organisations who helped them.

Also to be seen is an extensive picture of the county's part in the early days of flying, with exhibits ranging from the time of the First World War, through the stories of such aircraft as the infamous Flying Flea up to the jet age, for Britain's pioneering jet, the Gloster E.28/39, first took to the air at Cranwell. As the visitor will see, Lincolnshire's involvement with aviation's past extends to much more than the bomber offensive of 1939-45. Nonetheless, these few acres at East Kirkby played their part in the story of 'Bomber County' and it is surely fitting for 'Silksheen's' old Control Tower to be a prominent feature, along with her own 'Black Bullock'.

Above: The former Scampton gate guard, Lancaster NX611 re-assembled by an RAF team from Abingdon and in a completed state in the new hangar at East Kirkby during July 1988. *(W.J. Taylor)*

Below: Still carrying her 'Scampton' code YF:C, '611 is at her new home in 1989. In 1992 two codes were applied: 630's LE:C (port) and 57's DX:C (starboard). The lurid 'nose-art', (result of an MoD recruiting exercise) was later moved to the port side. *(W.P.Panton)*

Principal Units

Royal Air Force Station, East Kirkby
Station Commanders:
G/Capt R. T. Taafe OBE   20 Aug 43 - 30 Nov 44
G/Cpt B. A. Casey   1 Dec 44 - 30 Nov 45

No.55 Base, Bomber Command, RAF
Formed at East Kirkby, 15th April 1944. Disbanded in November 1945.
Base Commanders:
G/Capt R. T. Taafe OBE   15 Apr 44 - 15 May 44
Air Cmdr H. N. Thornton MBE
          15 May 44 - Jan 45
Air Cmdr R. W. Dickens DFC AFC
          Jan 45 - Oct 45
G/Capt B. A. Casey   Oct 45 - Nov 45

No.57 Squadron, RAF
Moved in from Scampton on 27th August 1943. Was disbanded on 27th November 1945 and re-formed at Scampton the following day.
Commanding Officers:
W/Cdr H. W. H. Fisher DFC   19 Aug 43 - 15 Apr 44
W/Cdr H. Y. Humphreys DFC 15 Apr 44 - 8 Jan 45
W/Cdr J. N. Tomes   8 Jan 45 - 12 Jun 45
W/Cdr D. M. Balme DSO DFC 12 Jun 45 - 18 Jun 45
W/Cdr H. Y. Humphreys DFC 18 Jun '45-23 Nov '45
W/Cdr M. W. Renaut   23 Nov 45
Aircraft flown: Avro Lancaster Mk.I, Mk.III
          Avro Lincoln B2
Aircraft Code: DX
R/T Call Sign: 'Acquire'

No.630 Squadron, RAF
The Squadron was formed at East Kirkby on 15th November 1943 and was disbanded there on 18th July 1945.
Commanding Officers:
W/Cdr M. Crocker DFC   15 Nov 43 - 12 Dec 43
W/Cdr J. D. Rollinson DFC   12 Dec 43 - 28 Jan 44
W/Cdr W. Deas DFC   1 Feb '44-7 Jul '44
W/Cdr L .M. Blome-Jones DFC
          12 Jul 44 - Sept 44
W/Cdr J. E. Grindon DFC   Sept 44 - Apr 45
W/Cdr F. W. L. Wild DFC   Apr 45 - 18 Jul 45

Aircraft flown: Avro Lancaster Mk.I, Mk.III
Aircraft Code: LE
R/T Call Sign: 'Gauntley'

No.460 Squadron, RAAF
Moved in from Binbrook on 27th July 1945 and was disbanded at East Kirkby on 10th October, 1945.
Commanding Officer:
W/Cdr P. H. Swann DSO DFC
Aircraft flown: Avro Lancaster Mk.I, Mk.III
Aircraft Code: AR

No.139 Squadron, RAF
Used East Kirkby airfield, on detachment from Coningsby, from the spring of 1946 until 4th February 1948.
Aircraft flown: De Havilland Mosquito B.IV
Aircraft Code: XD

No.231 OCU, RAF
Formed at Coningsby on 14th March 1947, and flew from East Kirkby airfield on detachment, from August 1947 until 4th February 1948.
Aircraft flown: Avro Anson, Airspeed Oxford
          DH Mosquito B.IV

7th Air Division, 3rd Air Force, USAF
3931st Air Base Group took over the station on 17th April 1954, handing it over to 3917th Air Base Group in July of that year. 3917th ABG acted as parent unit until 1st August 1958, when the USAF withdrew.

63rd Air Rescue Squadron.
Arrived from Norton Air Force Base on 3rd January 1955, left on 4th April 1955.

61st Air Rescue Squadron.
Arrived from Stead Air Force Base on 4th April 1955; left on 22nd June 1955.

64th Air Rescue Squadron.
Arrived on 22nd June 1955; left on 22nd September 1955.

Flying Douglas SC-47 aircraft, the three squadrons followed a 'Ninety Day Rotation' routine until mid-1958.

Wartime Operations carried out from East Kirkby

Date	Target/*Duty*	57 Sqn Desp	57 Sqn FTR	630 Sqn Desp	630 Sqn FTR	Date	Target/*Duty*	57 Sqn Desp	57 Sqn FTR	630 Sqn Desp	630 Sqn FTR
August 1943						**January 1944**					
30/31	Mönchen-gladbach	14	-			2/3	Berlin	10	2	11	-
31/						5/6	Stettin	8	1	13	-
Sep 1	Berlin	14	1			14/15	Brunswick	10	-	15	-
3/4	Berlin	14	1			20/21	Berlin	9	-	14	-
5/6	Mannheim	11	-			21/22	Magdeburg	9	-	13	-
6/7	Munich	9	-			27/28	Berlin	16	1	13	-
22/23	Hanover	22	-			28/29	Berlin	16	1	11	2
23/24	Mannheim	20	3			30/31	Berlin	14	-	10	-
27/28	Hanover	28	-								
29/30	Bochum	14	1			**February**					
						15/16	Berlin	19	-	21	1+1c
October						19/20	Leipzig	20	1	17	-
1/2	Hagen	14	-			20/21	Stuttgart	15	-	14	1+1c
2/3	Munich	15	1			24/25	Schweinfurt	18	1	16	-
3/4	Kassel	9	1			25/26	Augsburg	14	-	14	-
4/5	Frankfurt	12	1								
7/8	Stuttgart	20	-			**March**					
8/9	Hanover	14	-			1/2	Stuttgart	16	-	14	1
18/19	Hanover	21	-			10/11	Clermont-Ferrand	11	-	11	-
20/21	Leipzig	16	-			15/16	Stuttgart	21	-	20	2
22/23	Kassel	17	2			18/19	Frankfurt	19	-	18	1
						22/23	Frankfurt	19	-	15	-
November						24/25	Berlin	17	2	15	3
3/4	Dusseldorf	21	1			26/27	Essen	12	-	14	-
10/11	Modane	14	-			30/31	Nuremburg	18	1	16	3
18/19	Berlin	16	1c	9	-						
22/23	Berlin	14	-	10	-	**April**					
23/24	Berlin	12	-	10	2	5/6	Toulouse	12	-	9	-
26/27	Berlin	14	1	10	-	9/10	*Mining*	7	-	10	-
						10/11	Tours	14	-	17	-
December						11/12	Aachen	11	-	6	-
2/3	Berlin	14	2	13	1	18/19	Juvisy	18	1c	17	-
3/4	Leipzig	8	-	9	-	20/21	La Chapelle	16	1+1c	15	-
16/17	Berlin	15	1	12	-	22/23	Brunswick	16	-	15	-
20/21	Frankfurt	16	-	15	-	23/24	*Mining*		-	2	-
23/24	Berlin	12	1	12	-	24/25	Munich	16	-	16	1c
29/30	Berlin	15	1	15	-	26/27	Schweinfurt	14	2	15	1
						29/30	Clermont-Ferrand	13	-	12	-
January 1944						**May**					
1/2	Berlin	14	1	14	1	1/2	Tours	12	-	12	-

Date	Target/Duty	57 Sqn Desp	FTR	630 Sqn Desp	FTR
May					
3/4	Mailly-le-Camp	12	1	13	-
7/8	Tours	15	-	13	-
9/10	Annecy	11	-	10	-
11/12	Bourg Leopold	14	-	19	2
19/20	Amiens	16	-	18	-
21/22	Duisburg		-	5	1
	Stettin	3	-		
	Mining	12	1	14	1
22/23	Brunswick	16	3	16	-
24/25	Antwerp	12	-	11	-
27/28	St Valery-en-Caux	12	-	14	-
31/1	*Mining*	4	-		
June					
1/2	Saumur	15	-	15	-
3/4	Fermes	10	-		
4/5	Maisy	15	-	17	-
5/6	La Pernelle	16	-	15	-
6/7	Caen	14	-	13	1
7/8	Foret de Cerisey	11	-	13	-
9/10	Etampes	15	-	16	-
12/13	Caen	18	-	15	-
14/15	Aunay-sur-Odon	17	-	16	-
16/17	Beauvoir	19	-	19	-
21/22	Wesseling	18	6	19	4+1c
24/25	Ponnereval	9	-	13	-
27/28	Mimoyecques	13	-	16	-
July					
4/5	St Leu d'Esserant	17	2	20	1
7/8	St Leu d'Esserant	17	1	17	1
10/11	*Mining*	3	-	3	-
12/13	Calmont-Chalindry	13	-	11	-
14/15	Villeneuve-St Georges	9	-	9	-
15/16	Nevers	8	-	8	-
18	Caen	17	-	17	-
18/19	Revigny	10	1	10	4
19	Thivery (St Leu d'Esserant)	10	-	9	-
20/21	Courtrai	14	-	11	-
23/24	Kiel	6	-	6	-
	Mining	3	-	3	1
24/25	Stuttgart-	8	-	8	1
	St Nazaire	8	-	7	-
25/26	Stuttgart	12	-	12	-
26/27	Givors	10	-	8	-
28/29	Stuttgart	16	2	11	1
30	Cahagnes	13	-	12	-
	Rilly la-Montagnes	3	-		
31	Joigny La Roche	7	1	9	-
August					
1	Siracourt	6	-		
	La Breteque	2	-	4	-
2	Trossy St-Maximin	11	-	12	-
3	Trossy St-Maximin	8	-	10	-
5	St Leu d'Esserant	13	-	12	-
6	Foret d'Isle Adam	7	-		
	Bois de Cassan		-	6	-
7/8	Sequeville	13	-	14	1
9/10	Chatellerault	12	-	15	-
11	Bordeaux	5	-	5	-
11/12	Givors	8	-	10	-
12/13	Brunswick	9	-	8	-
	Falaise	4	-	3	-
14	Brest	8	-	4	-
15	Deelen	14	-	11	-
16/17	Stettin	9	-	13	1
18	Foret d'Isle-Adam	9	-	5	1
	Bordeaux	9	-	1	-
18/19	*Mining*	4	-		
20/21	Brest	4	-		
25/26	Darmstadt	16	1	15	-
26/27	Königsberg	15	2	14	-
29/30	Königsberg		-	12	-
	Mining			4	-
31	Bergueneuse	13	-	15	-
September					
2	Brest	12	1	11	-
3	Deelen	17	-	17	-
9/10	Mönchen-gladbach	14	-	16	-
11	Le Havre	14	-	11	-
11/12	Darmstadt	17	-	17	-
12/13	Stuttgart	15	-	13	-
17	Boulogne	17	-	17	-
18/19	Bremerhaven	19	1	16	-
19/20	Mönchen-gladbach	17	-	17	-
23/24	Hansdorf/Munster	18	-	21	-
26/27	Karlsruhe	19	-	20	-
27/28	Kaiserslkautern	21	-	19	-
29	*Mining*	5	-		
October					
5	Wilhelmshaven	20	-	21	-
6	Bremen	18	-	18	-
	Mining	2	-	3	-
7	Flushing	16	-	16	-
	Mining	5	-		
11	Veere	9	-		

Left table

Date	Target/Duty	57 Sqn Desp	FTR	630 Sqn Desp	FTR
October					
14/15	Brunswick	20	-	20	-
15/16	*Mining*			2	-
17	Walcheren	6	-	5	-
19/20	Nuremburg	21	-	20	-
23	Flushing	6	-	6	-
24/25	*Mining*	4	-	4	-
28/29	Bergen	20	-	19	-
30	Walcheren	9	-	12	-
November					
1	Homburg	21	-	19	-
2/3	Dusseldorf	17	-	14	-
4/5	Ladburgen	13	-	14	-
6	Graavenhorst	17	1		
11/12	Harburg	16	1	17	
	Mining	3	-	2	-
16	Duren	18	-	19	-
21/22	Gravenhorst	20	-	21	-
22/23	Trondheim	13	-	12	1c
26/27	Munich	14	-	20	-
December					
4/5	Heilbron	20	1	20	-
6/7	Giessen	15	2	16	-
8	Urftdam	14	-	14	1
10	Urftdam	14	-		
11	Urftdam	17	1	15	-
14	*Mining*			2	-
17/18	Munich	18	2	17	-
	Lutzow	2	-		
18/19	Gydnia	10	-	13	-
	Mining	2	-	3	-
21/22	Politz	6	-	6	-
26	St Vith	2	-	2	-
28/29	*Mining*	3	-	3	-
31	Houffalize	13	-	12	-
	Mining			2	1
January 1945					
1	Ladburgen	10	-	10	-
1/2	Gravenhorst	8	-	6	-
4/5	Royan	16	-1c	18	-
5/6	Houffalize	14	-	9	-
6/7	*Mining*			3	-
7/8	Munich	15	-	14	1c
13/14	Politz	12	-	15	1
	Mining	3	-	3	-
14/15	Merseburge	15	-	13	-
16/17	Brux	9	-	15	-
February					
1/2	Siegen	18	-	19	-

Right table

Date	Target/Duty	57 Sqn Desp	FTR	630 Sqn Desp	FTR
February					
2/3	Karlsruhe	17	-	16	-
7/8	Ladburgen	15	-	12	-
8/9	Politz	19	1	19	-
13/14	Dresden	18	-	17	-
14/15	Rositz	16	-	14	1
19/20	Bolen	16	-	15	-
20/21	Mittelland/ Gravenhorst	11	-	11	-
21/22	Gravenhorst	13	-	13	-
23	*Mining*	1	-	2	-
24	Ladburgen	13	-	13	-
March					
3/4	Ladburgen	15	-	13	-
5/6	Bohlen	21	-	17	-
6/7	Sassnitz	16	-	11	-
	Mining			3	-
7/8	Harburg	16	1	15	-
11	Essen	11	-	15	-
11/12	*Mining*	2	-	2	-
12	Dortmund	17	-	16	-
14/15	Lutzkendorf	17	-	15	-
16/17	Wurzburg	14	-	18	1
20/21	Bohlen	15	1+1c	19	-
21/22	Hamburg	11	-	16	-
23/24	Wesel	13	-	17	-
April					
4	Noordhausen	18	-	17	-
6	Molbis			11	-
8/9	Lutzkendorf	18	-	17	1c
10/11	Leipzig	18	-	11	2
13/14	*Mining*			4	-
16/17	Pilsen	14	-	14	-
23	Flensburg (abandoned)	12	-	12	-
25	Berchtesgaden	5	-	5	-
25/26	*Mining*	4	-	4	-

KEY:

Desp - Aircraft Despatched
FTR - Failed to Return
c - Crashed

Squadron Awards

Awards to No.57 Squadron
1939 - 1945

Distinguished Service Order
W/Cdr F. C. Hopcroft DFC   S/Ldr J. Vivien DFC

Bar to Distinguished Flying Cross
P/O M. E. Walsh DFC   S/Ldr J. H. Leland DFC
S/Ldr G. W. Curry DFC   S/Ldr R. E. S. Smith DFC

Distinguished Flying Cross

F/Lt G. M. Wyatt	F/O E. W. G. Rosam
P/O W. C. Hutchings	P/O W. W. Griffin
F/O A. J. Smitz	P/O S. Danahy
S/Ldr M. V. Peters-Smith	L. F. Shepherd
P/O E. C. Cox	S/Ldr G. G. Avis
P/O W. L. Jennings	P/O A. M. Singer
P/O E. H. O'Neill	P/O P. L. Singer
P/O J. E. Swift	F/Lt C. V. Ciano
S/Ldr P. H. Wray	F/Lt W. E. Roberts
P/O G. C. Andrew	F/Lt A. E. W. Wynyard
P/O R. F. L. Tong	P/O E. W. Lovejoy
S/Ldr E. A. Warfield	P/O L. E. McKenzie
F/Lt G. R. Watson	S/Ldr L. J. Birchall
P/O E. A. Hudson	F/Lt A. J. A. Day
F/O M. Blank	F/Lt J. M. Greig
W/O W. C. Vanexan	F/Lt R. W. Stewart
F/Lt W. E. Blench	F/O M. R. McCullagh
P/O L. F. Austin	F/O N. W. C. Mould
P/O M. E. Walsh	P/O R. P. Grimwood
S/Ldr D. G. Long	F/Lt J. C. Anderson
F/O E. W. Adams	P/O J. B. King
F/O F. Carter	F/Lt G. H. Laing
F/O E. W. Patteson	F/O W. T. Hasby
F/O C. Shaw	P/O S. C. Atcheson
P/O MacDonald	S/Ldr M. I. Boyle
W/O E. T. English	P/O A. W. Fearn
W/O J. Tough	F/Lt R. V. Munday
F/O P. Robins	F/Lt R. K. Eggins
S/Ldr M. Crocker	F/O F. A. Thomas
P/O J. A. Brown	F/Lt J. S. Ludford
F/Lt P. Whittam	F/O H. H. Chadwick

P/O H. S. Gifford	F/O G. K. King
P/O T. G. L. Irwin	P/O J. Sheriff
P/O L. W. J. King	P/O D. A. West
P/O W. E. McCrae	P/O E. A. Dowland
F/Lt A. F. Gobbie	F/Lt J. Simms
P/O K. H. Ryrie	F/O R. Davies
P/O S. G. Stevens	P/O G. S. Collins
P/O J. T. Agnew	P/O T. Davies
F/O B. P. McGonagle	P/O G. J. M. Martin
F/Lt E. T. Hodgkinson	F/Lt D. H. Reid
F/O R. McRobbie	F/Lt K. D. Smith
P/O R. J. Gooch	P/O R. E. Walker
P/O E. H. Howes	F/O I. P. Mapp
P/O J. B. Josling	P/O A. E. Nicklin
P/O A. R. Knowles	W/Cdr H. Y. Humphries
P/O F. Norcliffe	F/O C. S. Paton
P/O W. H. H. Siddons	F/O G. Pow
P/O S. G. Townsend	F/O H. Welland
P/O J. A. Kimber	F/O H. B. MacKinnon
F/O J. C. Lumsden	F/O C. V. Allen
W/O P. V. Hazeldene	F/O M. O. Clarke
F/Lt P. Ainley	F/O J. S. Beard
F/O A. C. MacKellar	F/O J. MacDonald
S/Ldr D. I. Fairbairn	P/O C. Shillaw
F/Lt E. C. W. Anderson	F/O J. H. C. Braham
F/O J. Castagnola	F/Lt J. C. Warburton
F/O K. E. Bly	F/Lt W. M. Watt
F/O W. F. Martin	F/Lt L. W. Ottewell
F/O O. W. Thomas	F/O J. Vasey
F/O A. Ross	P/O A. H. Moores
F/Lt P. A. Bennett	F/Lt E. Blanchard
F/O A. V. H. Wardle	F/O O. G. Thomas
F/O J. H. Jackson	F/O Clark DFM
F/Lt L. T. A. Mersh	F/Lt L. C. Slade
W/O Warsop	

Member of the British Empire
F/O W. H. G. Hampshire

Conspicuous Gallantry Medal
F/Sgt W. H. Cowham

Bar to the Distinguished Flying Medal
F/Sgt R. Roberts DFM

Awards to No. 630 Squadron 1943 - 1945

Distinguished Flying Medal

Cpl S. Culver
Sgt A. C. Thomas
Cpl A. Daley
Sgt F. R. Connor
Sgt G. H. A. Polson
Sgt S. R. Frost
Sgt F. C. Sergent
Sgt H. A. Taylor
Sgt G. H. Dow
Sgt H. G. Lines
Sgt R. Durham
Sgt A. G. Maskell
F/Sgt V. S. Moore
F/Sgt T. H. Donelly
Sgt P. F. H. Hawkins
Sgt E. W. Keene
Sgt J. B. Price
Sgt J. L. T. Williams
Sgt F. J. Jones
F/Sgt A. B. Welford
Sgt R. W. Lovell
Sgt S. J. Mondell
F/Sgt K. Finch
F/Sgt C. W. Glencross
F/Sgt J. B. Hughes
Sgt D. J. Griffiths
F/Sgt W. L. Bell
F/Sgt J. A. Thomas

F/Sgt F. Carter
F/Sgt F. K. Evans
Sgt E. Jenkins
F/Sgt J. D. Dickson
F/Sgt J. H. P. Dwyer
Sgt R. W. R.Grellier
F/Sgt J. McB Dempster
F/Sgt R. Croston
Sgt E. Broadbent
F/Sgt J. W. Colbert
F/Sgt R. Crossgrove
F/Sgt I. L. McCall
F/Sgt K. J. Stevens
F/Sgt W. Woodhouse
F/Sgt D. G. Lightfoot
F/Sgt W. Davis
F/Sgt H. Johnson
Sgt F. H. Simmonds
Sgt J. T. Watts
F/Sgt R. W. Cleary
Sgt F. D. Roberts
Sgt R .D. Chandler
Sgt J. C. Evans
F/Sgt R. A .Hammersley
F/Sgt P. S Baker
Sgt L. J. Champion
F/Sgt J. F. Gauweloose
F/Sgt M. J. Thorne

Croix de Guerre (Belgium)
W/O C. J. Woodrow

Mention must be made of 57 Squadron's Commanding Officer at the outbreak of the Second World War.

Wing Commander H. M. A. Day GC DSO OBE was shot down and taken prisoner on the Squadron's first operation of that war, on 13th October, 1939. Nine times he got away, only to be recaptured each time. At other times he assisted others to escape and at the end of the war was instrumental in saving a number of important captives from the hands of the SS and Gestapo. For these exploits he was awarded the DSO and OBE. (He had been awarded the Albert Medal for saving life many years before; this was converted to the George Cross later.) His career is recorded fully in *Wings Day*, by Sydney Smith.

Note: No official lists of awards to members of either squadron exist. The lists shown were compiled after a search through Squadron Records and the weekly issues of *The Aeroplane*, September 1939 to December 1945. Unfortunately, in the latter source, names were not always accompanied by squadron numbers, so it is inevitable that there are omissions.

Distinguished Service Order
W/Cdr J. E. Grindon DFC

Second Bar to Distinguished Flying Cross
S/Ldr R. O. Calvert DFC   S/Ldr E. R. Butler DFC

Bar to Distinguished Flying Cross
W/Cdr M. Crocker DFC   F/Lt K. R. Ames DFC

Distinguished Flying Cross

F/Lt D. A. MacDonald
F/Lt D. S. Paterson
P/O A. E. A. Mathews
P/O J. R. Worthington
P/O A. H. Gidson
F/Lt J. C. W. Weller
F/O C. H. Johnson
F/O H. M. MacDonald
F/Lt W. H. Kellaway DSO
F/Lt T. Neilson
P/O R. C. Hooper
F/O J. H. Pratt
F/O A. G. Blois
P/O T. Smart
W/O L. H. Todd
P/O R. T. Hughes
F/O G. W. Brake
P/O F. R. G. A. Higgins
P/O H. Glasby
F/O D. Roberts
F/O H. H. Long
F/O R. L. McCann
F/O D. R. Mallinson
F/O M. A. Swain
F/O E. P. Mitchell
F/O A. R. Kerr
P/O W. K. Goodhew
F/Lt T. G. O'Dwyer
F/Lt G. K. W. Arkieson
F/O H. A. Ramsey

F/O A. J. Wright
F/O G. H. Probert
F/Lt H. W. Hill
F/Lt F. D. Spencer
F/O H. G. Rogers
P/O A. J. Lucas
P/O A. J. Payne
F/O A. Kuzma
F/O K. G. Chamberlain
F/O A. W. G. Connor DFM
F/O W. Mooney DFM
P/O L. N. Rackley
S/Ldr Millichap
F/Lt J. W. Martin
F/Lt N. A. G. Beaudoin
F/Lt L. H. Wood
F/O G. J. Bate
F/O J. W. Lennon
F/O D. E. Hawker
W/Cdr L. M. Blome-Jones
W/O G. A. Whitley
F/Lt H. D. Archer
Lt M. T. Ackerman
F/Lt R. K. Foulkes
F/O F. E. H. Millar
F/O N. E. Westergaard
F/Lt L. Ovens
F/Lt S. A. Nunns
F/Lt T. B. Baker

Distinguished Flying Medal

F/Sgt J. White
F/Sgt J. G. L. Martin
Sgt R. S. Parle
Sgt P. W. Vaggs
Sgt D. J. Taylor
F/Sgt A. W. Jeffrey
F/Sgt M. Barry

F/Sgt T. H. Savage
F/Sgt G. A. Davies
F/Sgt D. W. Allen
F/Sgt W. E. J. Cox
F/Sgt E. J. Browne
F/Sgt H. McDonald

British Empire Medal
F/Sgt D. S. Morgan

Bibliography

After the Battle - facsimile maps.

The Airfields of Lincolnshire since 1912, Ron Blake, Mike Hodgson and Bill Taylor, Midland Counties Publications, Leicester, 1984.

*Bomber Command, Max Hastings, Michael Joseph, London, 1979.

The Bomber Command War Diaries: An Operational Reference Book 1939-45, Martin Middlebrook and Chris Everitt, Viking, London, 1985.

Bomber Intelligence, W.E.Jones, Midland Counties Publications, 1983.

Bomber Offensive, Sir Arthur T.Harris, Collins, London, 1947.

Bomber Offensive, Anthony Verrier, London, 1968.

Enemy Coast Ahead, Guy Gibson.

Lancaster: Story of a Famous Bomber, Bruce Robertson, Harleyford.

Lancaster at War 1, 2, 3, Mike Garbett and Brian Goulding, Ian Allan, London.

Magazines: *The Aeroplane, Flight, Flypast*.

*The Mighty Eighth, Roger Freeman, Arms & Armour Press, London, 1989.

Mosquito Squadrons of the RAF, Chaz Bowyer, Ian Allan, London, 1984.

No.5 Bomber Group, W.J.Lawrence, Faber, London, 1951.

The Nuremburg Raid, Martin Middlebrook, Allen Lane, London.

*Squadrons of the Royal Air Force & Commonwealth 1918-88, James J.Halley, Air-Britain, 1988.

Story of a Lanc, Brian Goulding, Mike Garbett and John Partridge.

Strike Force, Robert Jackson, Robson Books, London, 1986.

* At the time of going to press, these particular titles are still available (usually in a later edition than that quoted) from Midland Counties Publications' mail order service.

Aviation and Military Books by Post

We stock many thousands of Aviation, Military, Spaceflight, Astronomy, Railway and Road Transport books (and videos) from all over the world, for world-wide mail order.

Our quick turn-round and superb packing is unrivalled.

Free informative and illustrated catalogue (specify interest areas) on request - Write or phone -

Midland Counties Publications,
Unit 3, Maizefield, Hinckley Fields,
Hinckley, Leics. LE10 1YF.

Telephone: 0455 233 747; Fax: 0455 841 805